Country Roads ~ the Monadnocks

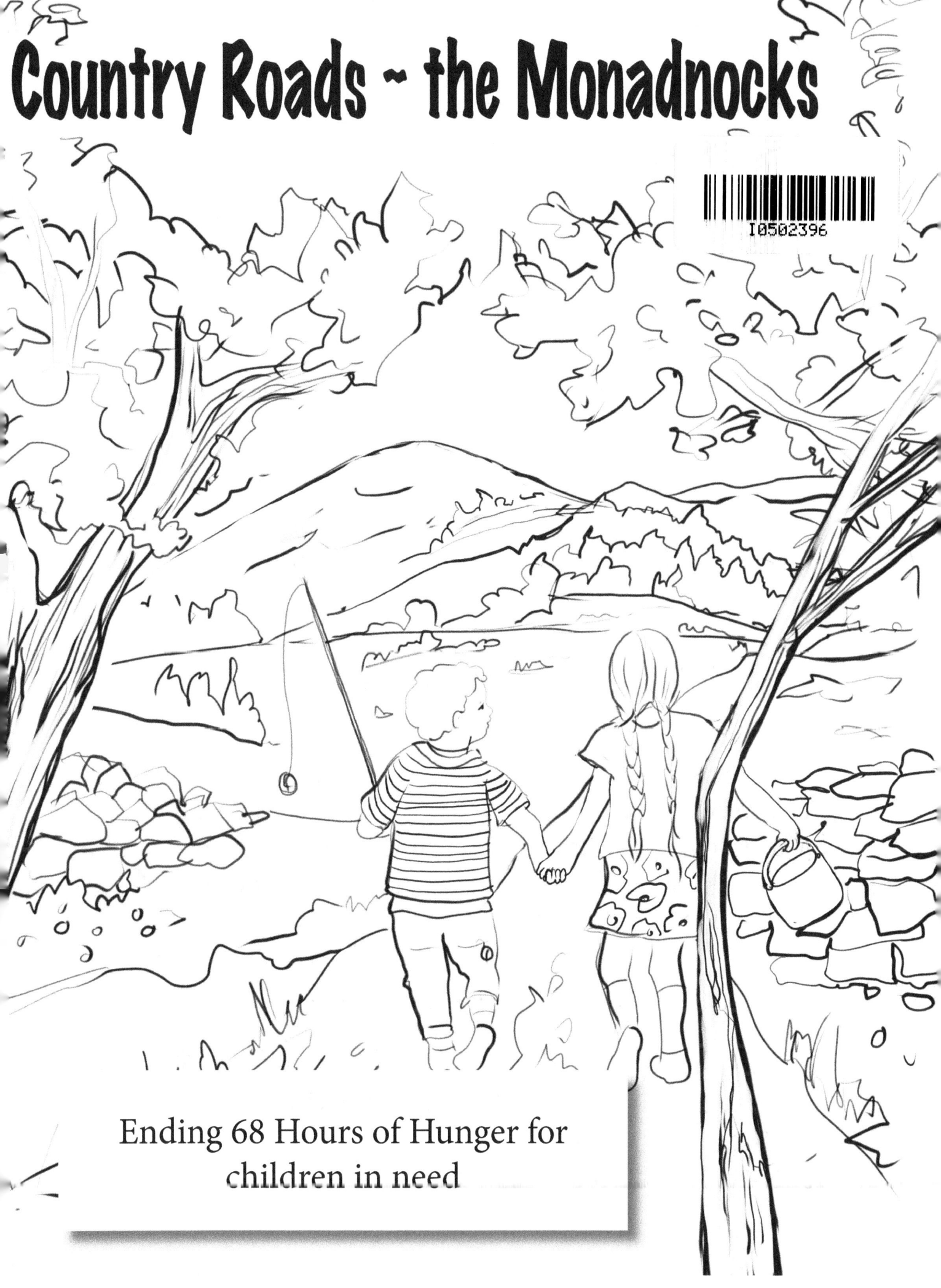

I0502396

Ending 68 Hours of Hunger for children in need

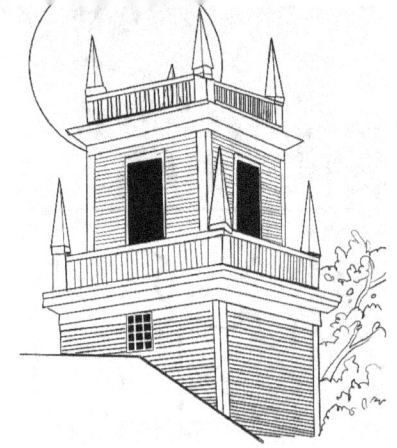

Supporting the program to:
End 68 Hours of Hunger
(website for information: end68hoursofhunger.org)

Country Roads ~ The Monadnocks
copyright © 2017 Union Congregational Church, UCC

Published by the Union Congregational Church, UCC
in the United States of America
ISBN-13: 978-1545382165
ISBN-10: 1545382166

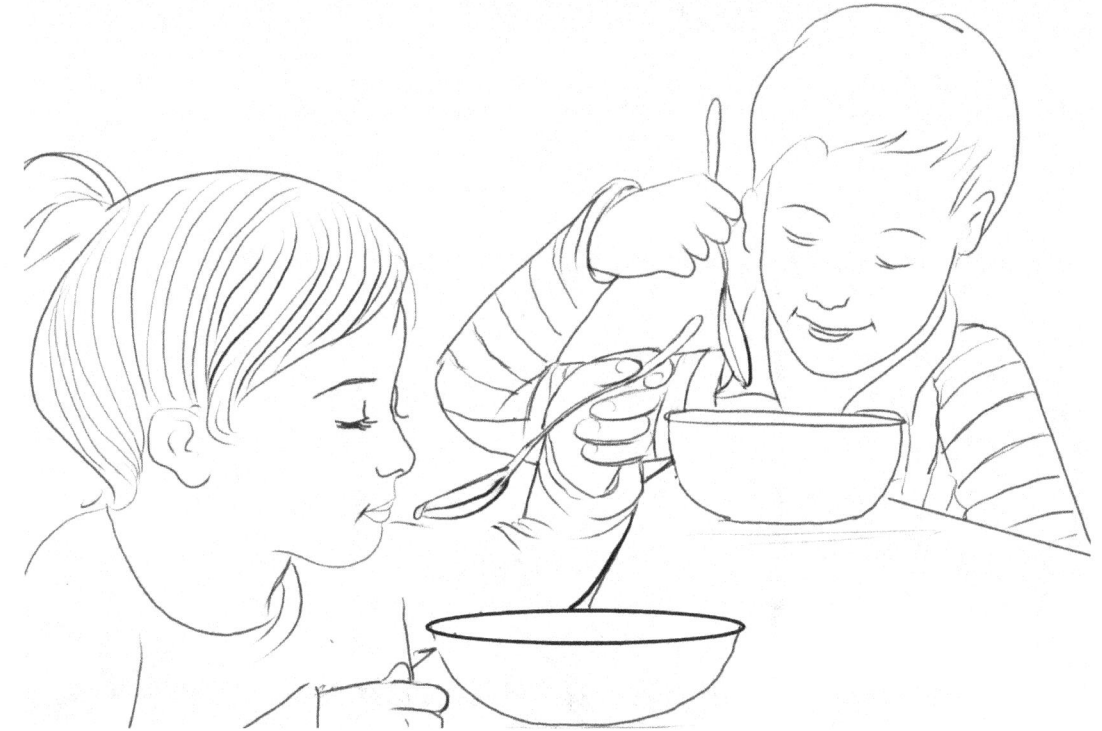

Thank you for purchasing this coloring book. It is designed for all ages, with some images being more challenging than others.

If you work as a family, the book can be great fun and knowing that all the money from each book is helping to fund the ConVal School District program to END 68 HOURS OF HUNGER is an added blessing.

The program is a private, not-for-profit, effort to confront the approximately 68 hours of hunger that some schoolchildren experience between the free lunch they receive on Friday afternoon and the free breakfast they receive in school on Monday morning.

Apple Picking in the Monadnock Region

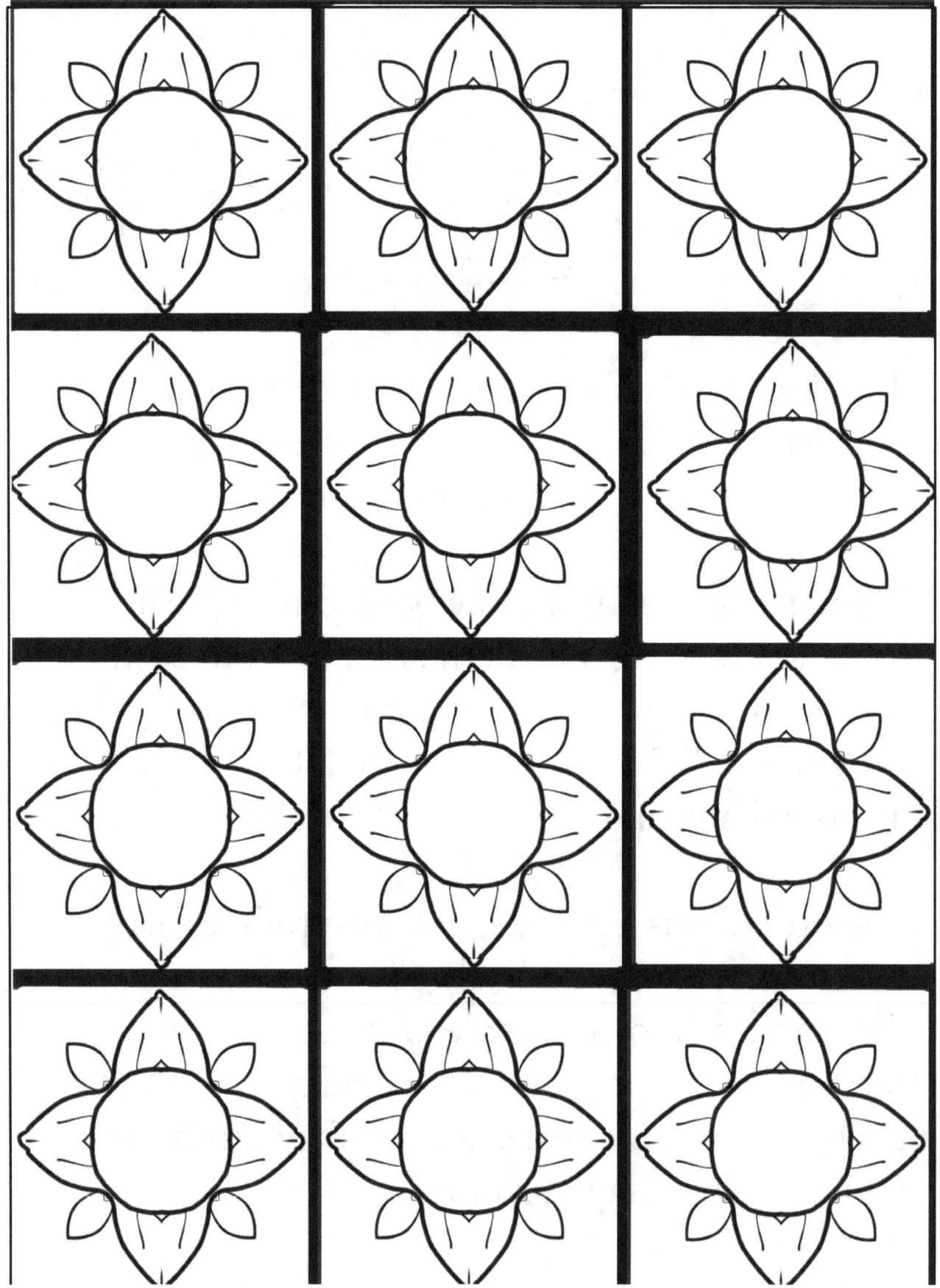

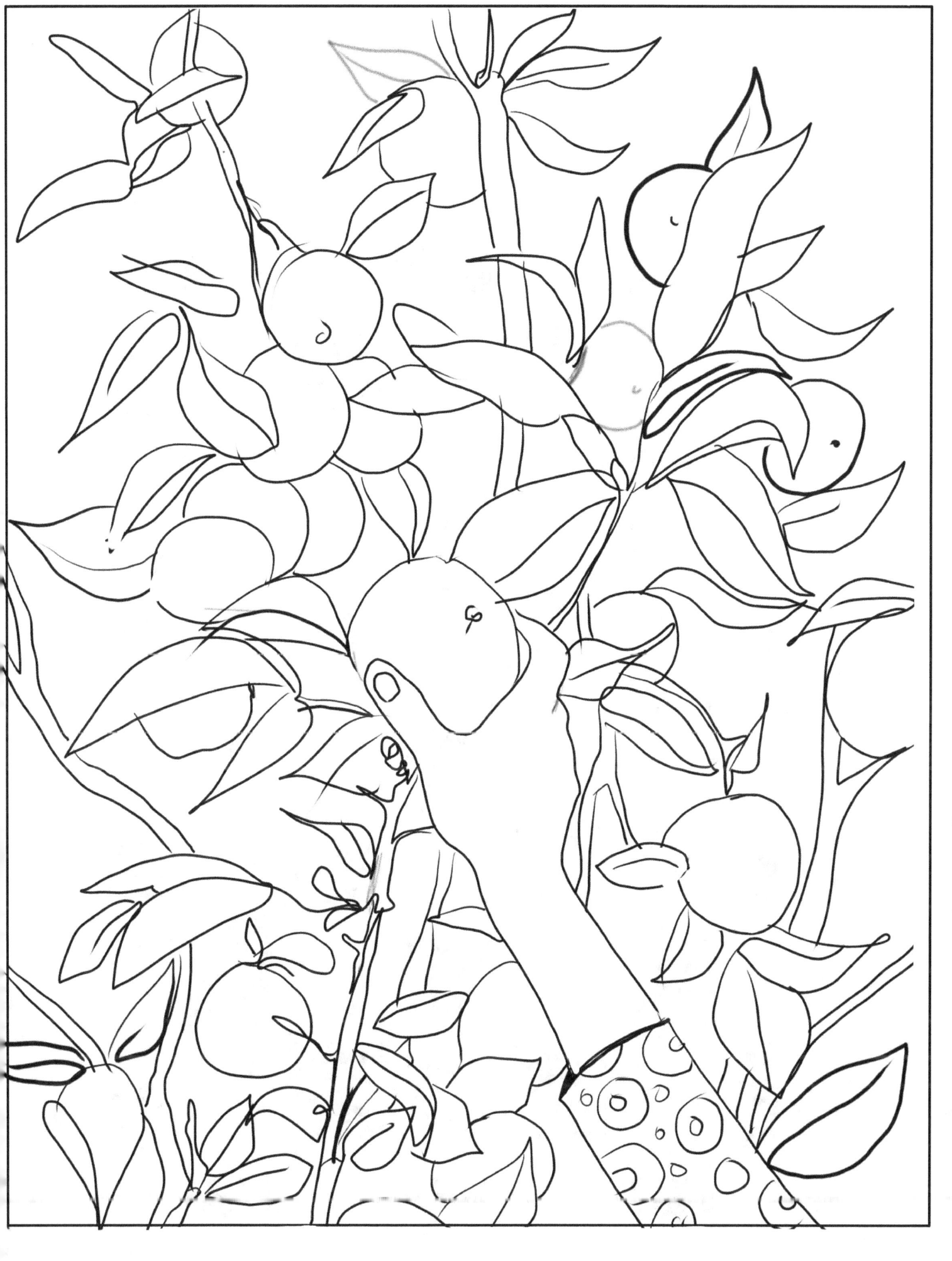

Who let the dogs loose?

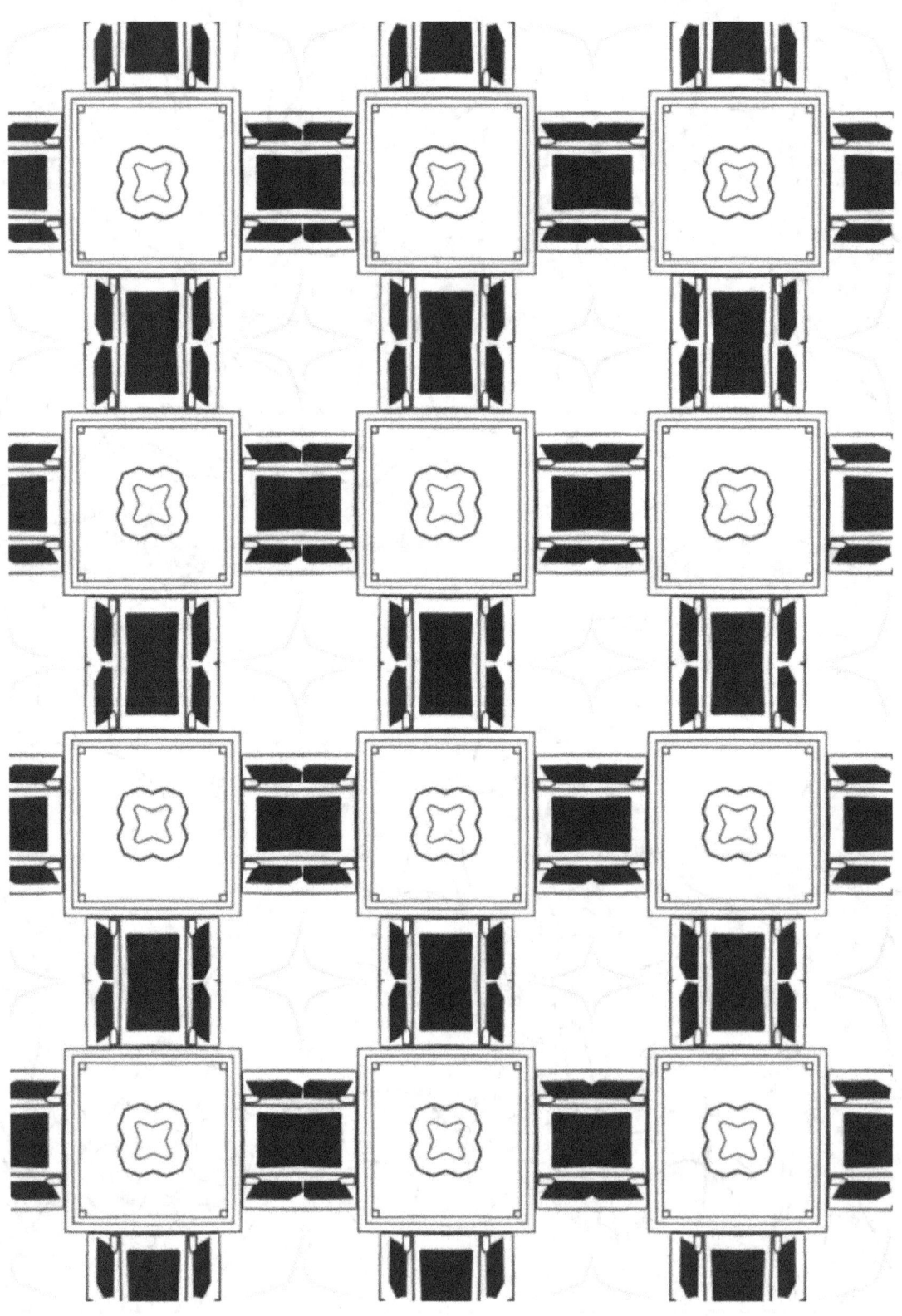

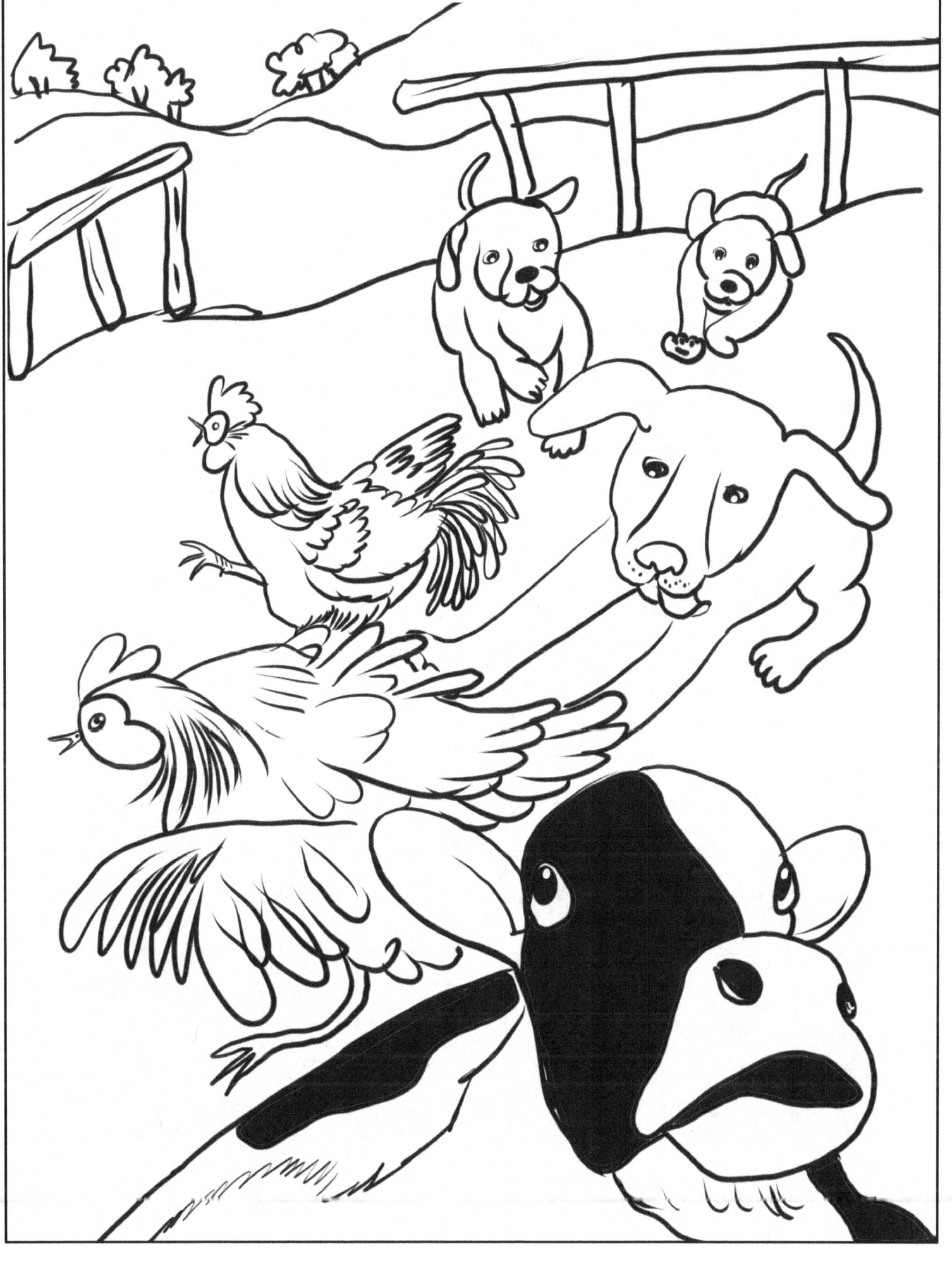

A Cairn, or Rock Sculpture on the Water

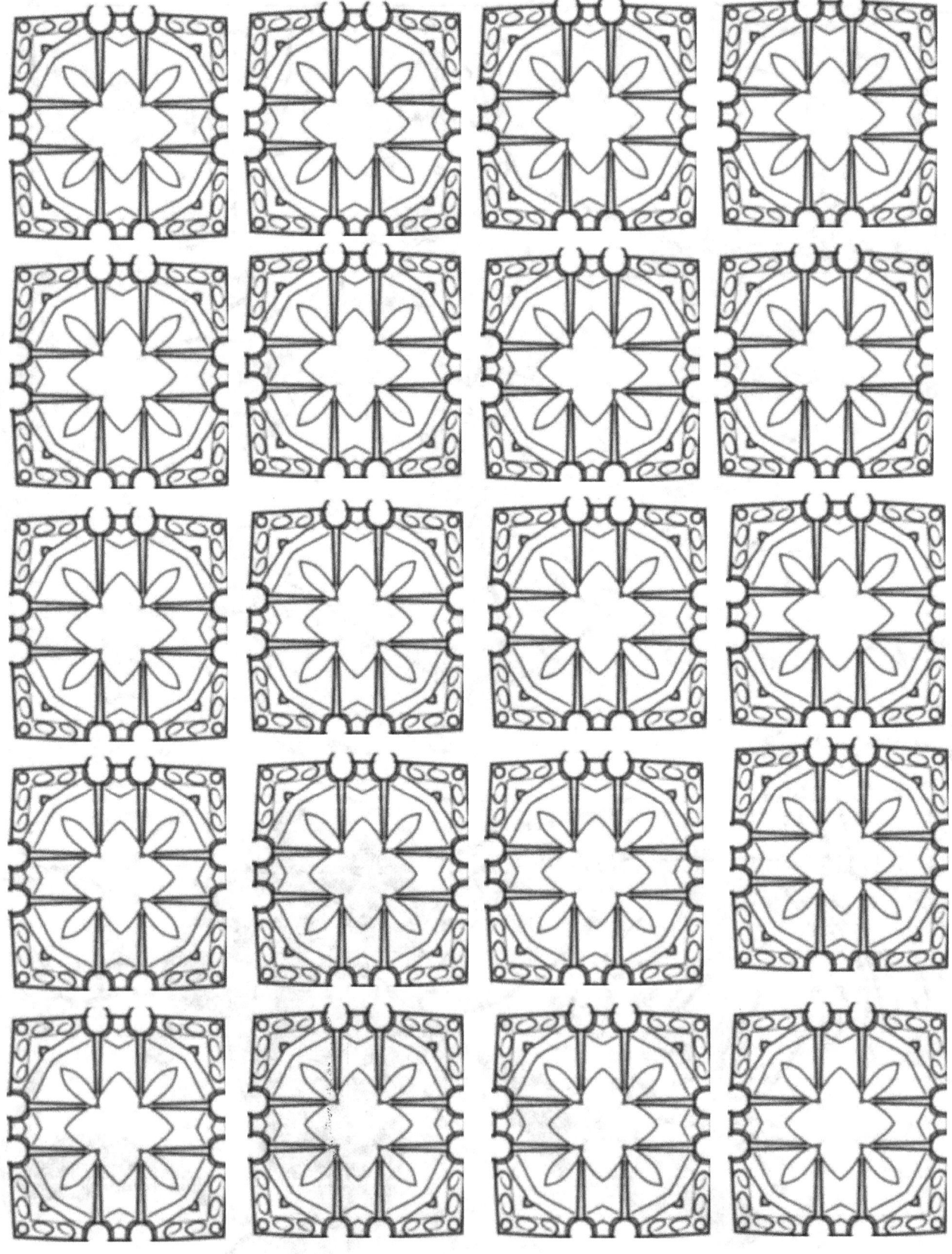

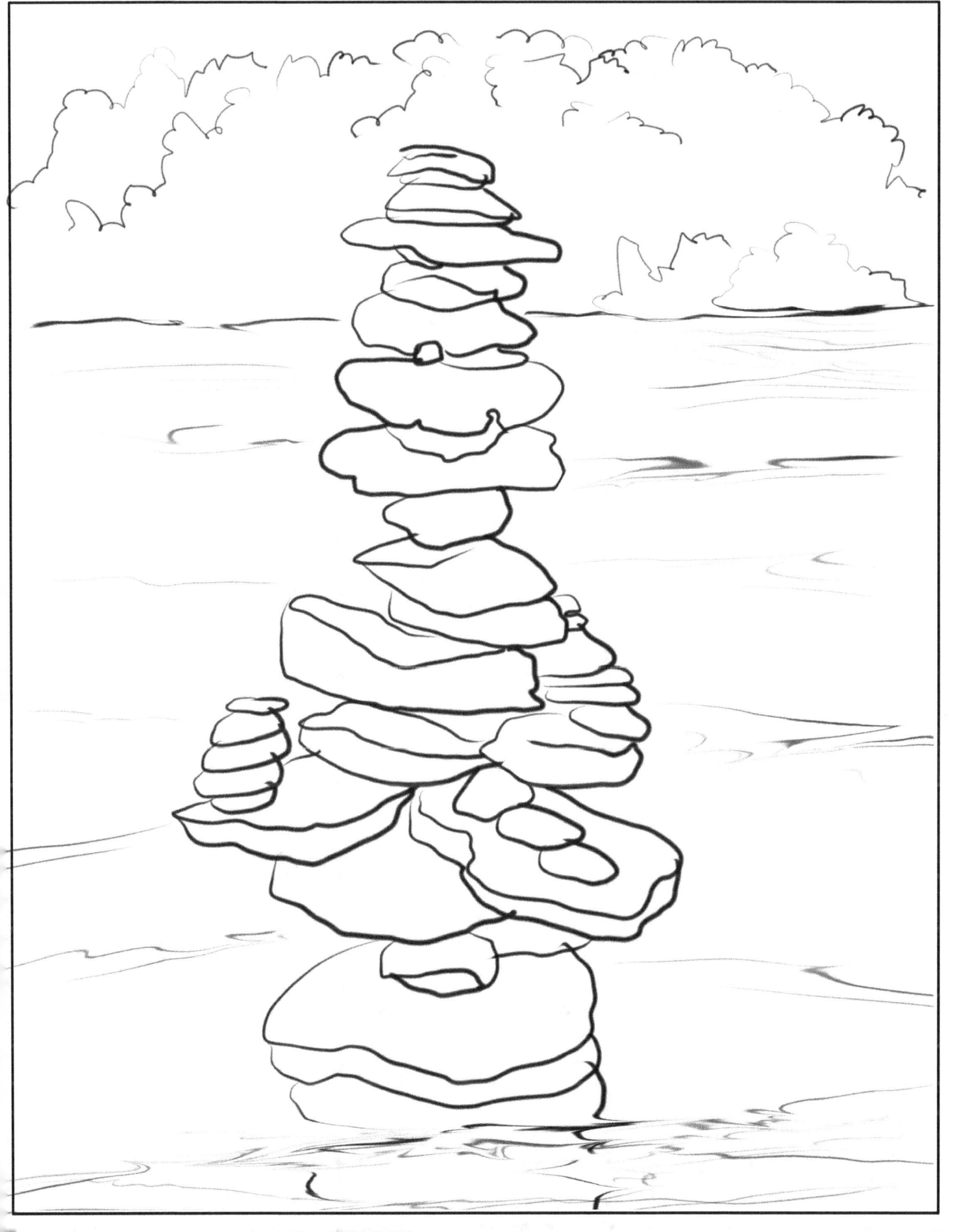

The Cathedral of the Pines in Rindge, NH

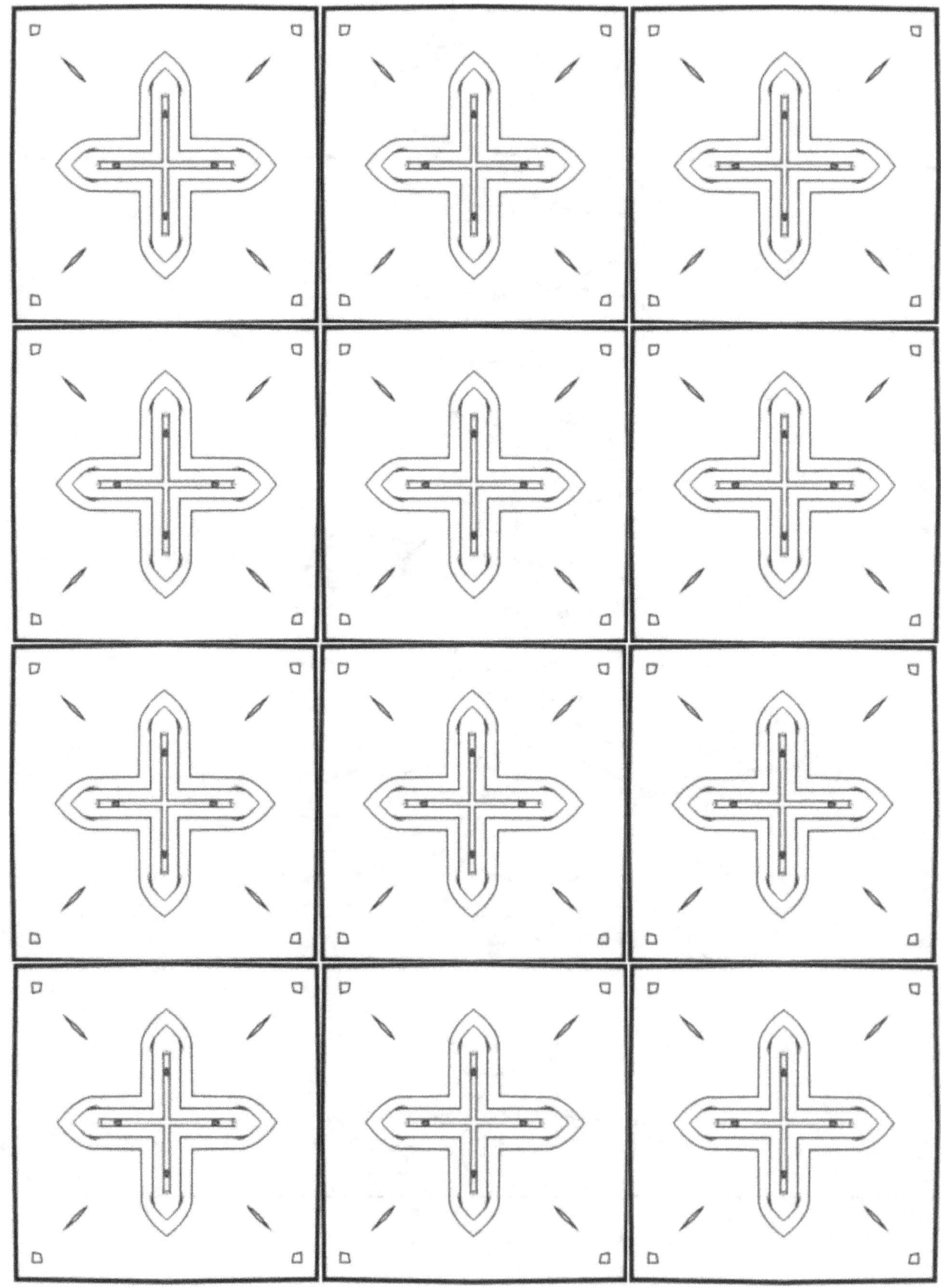

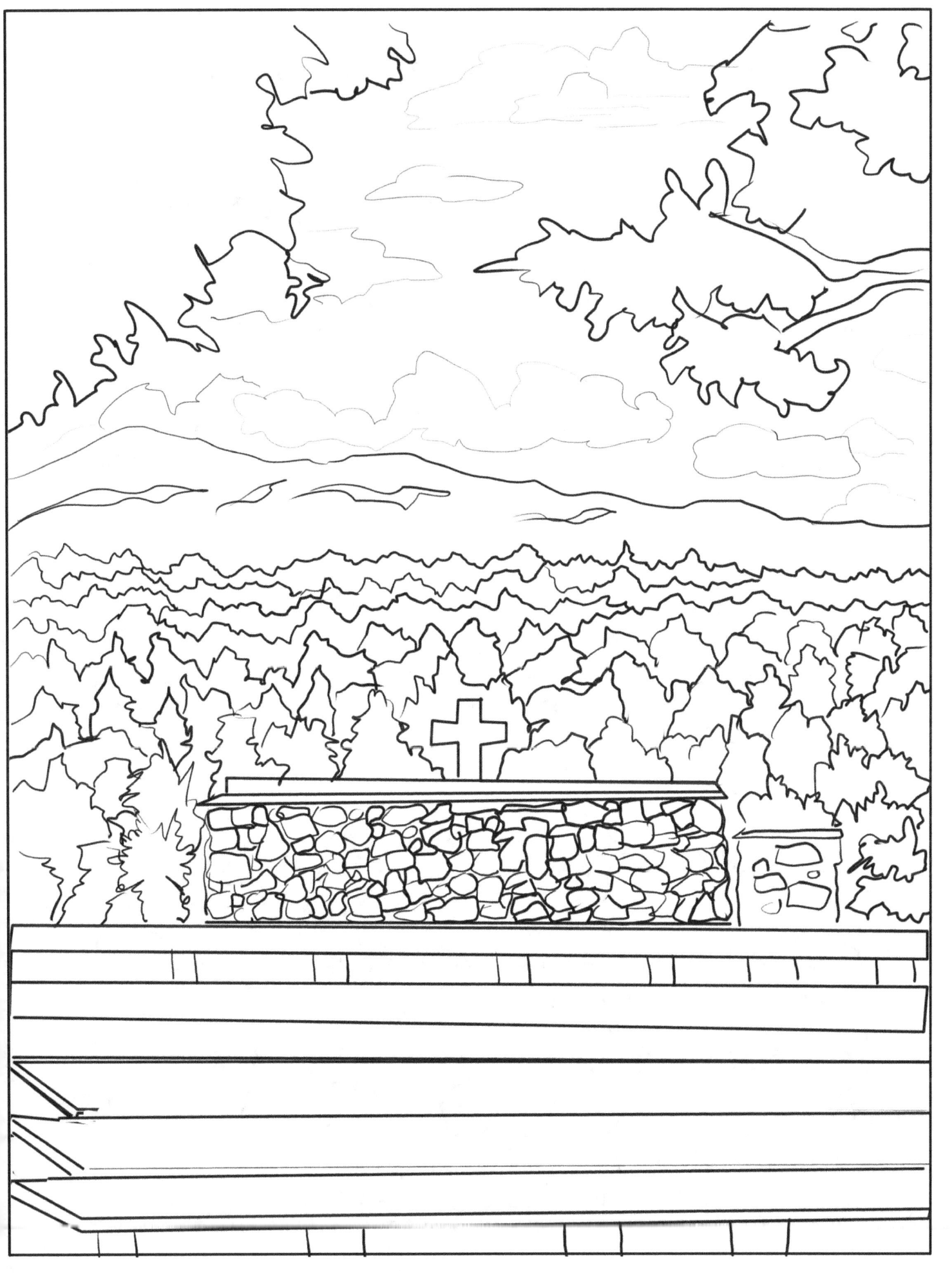

Fill your bucket near a mountainside stream.

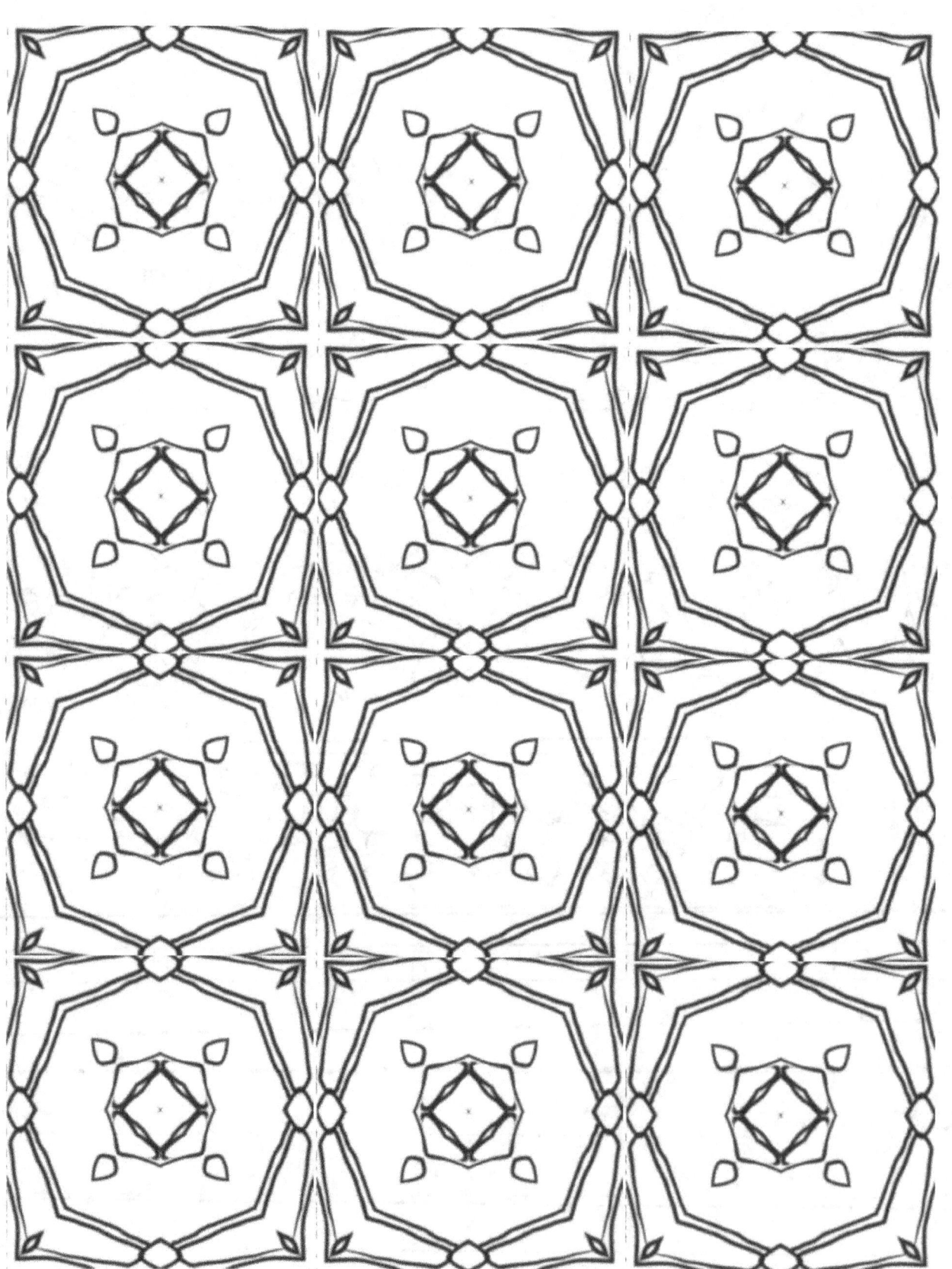

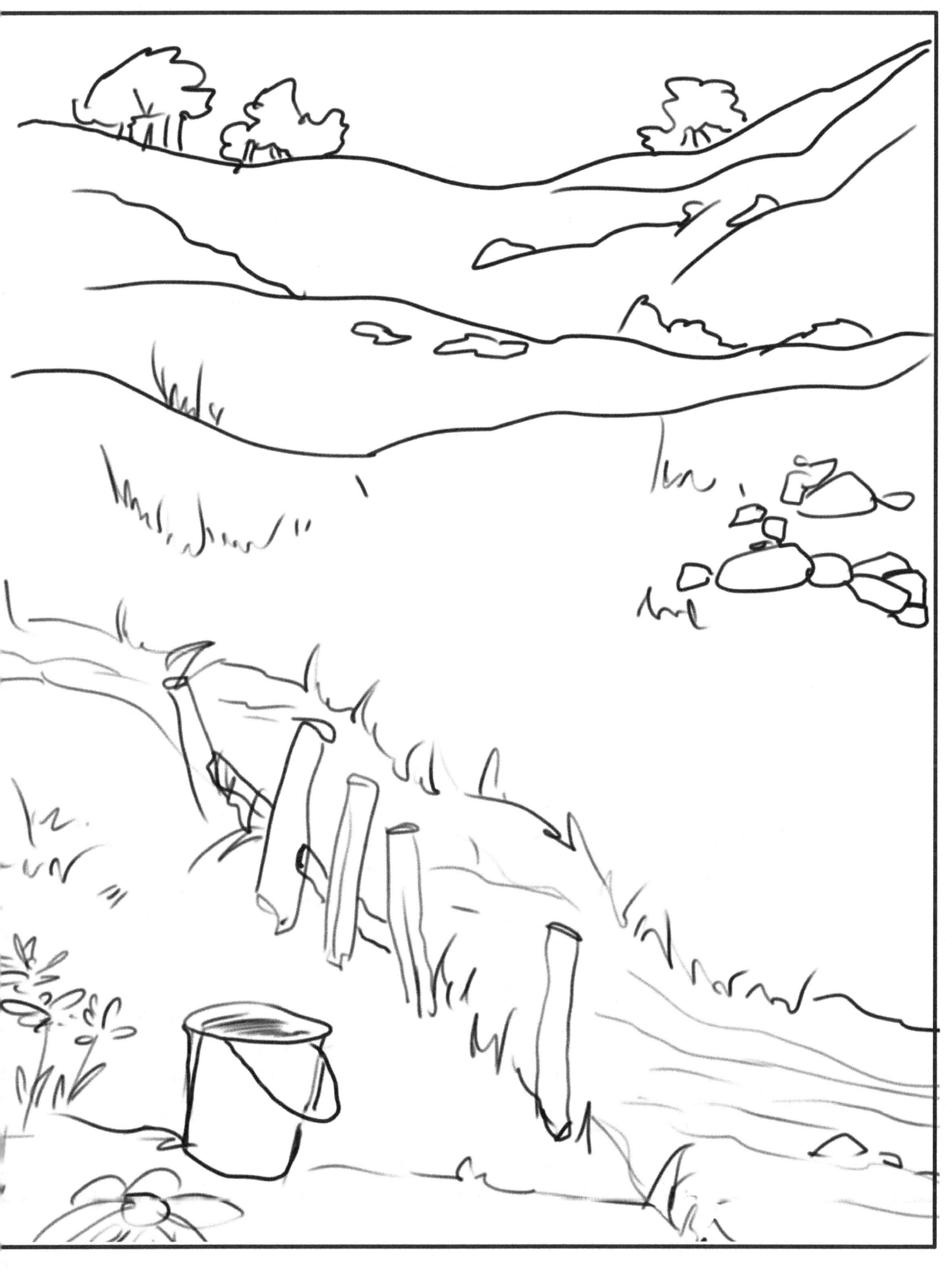

The Monadnock Area is home to many deer.

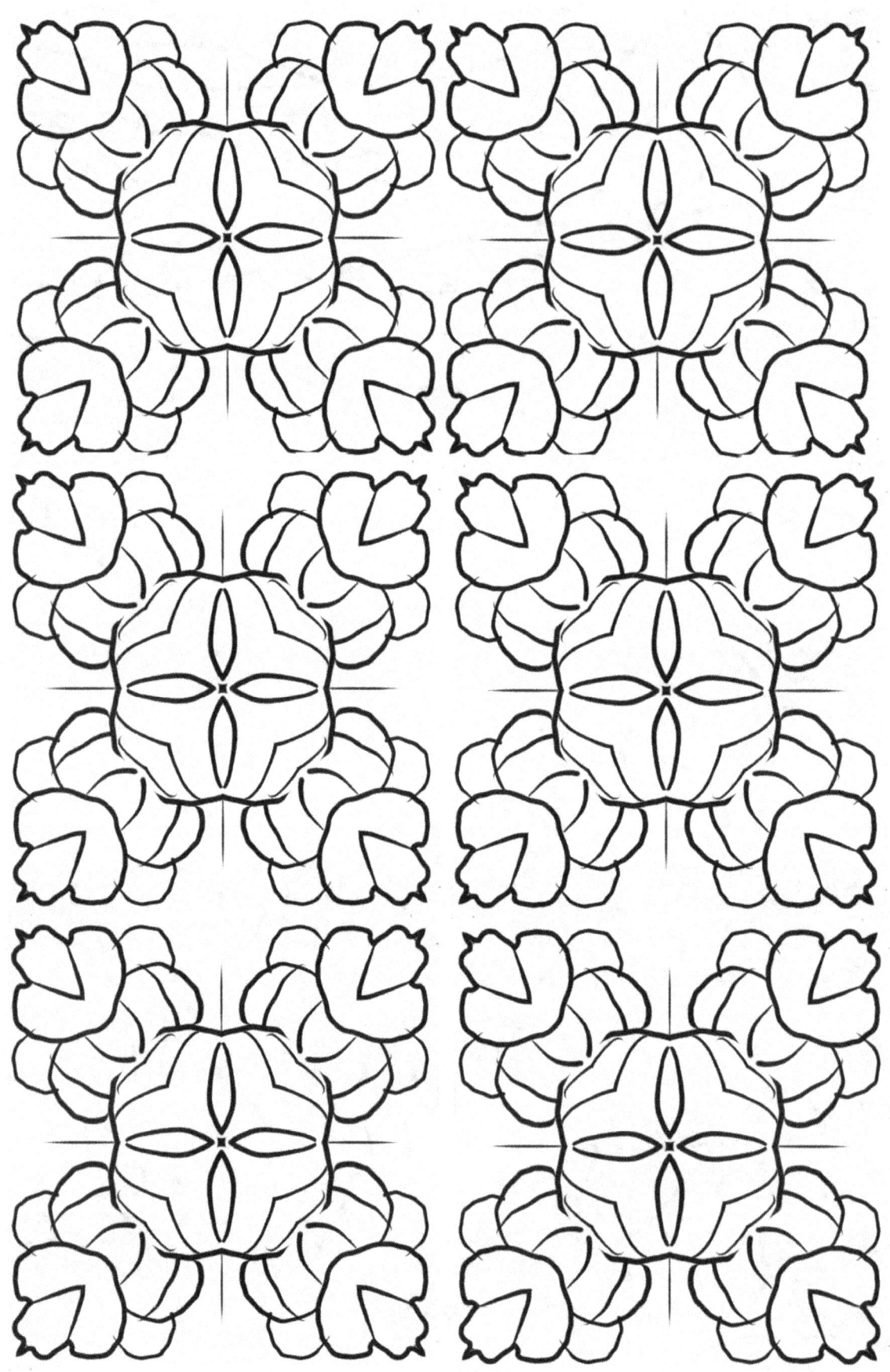

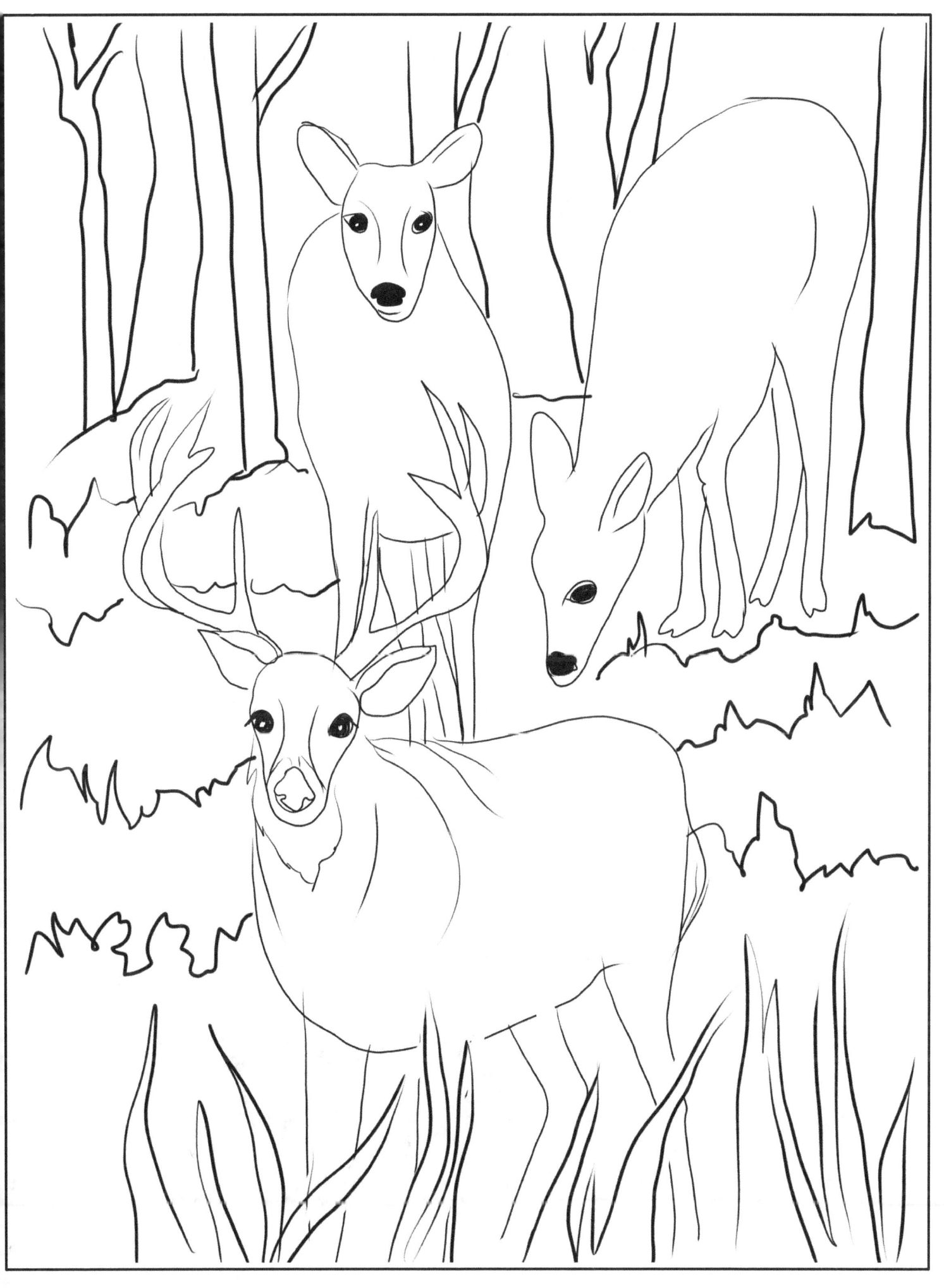

Everyone helps out when you live on a farm.

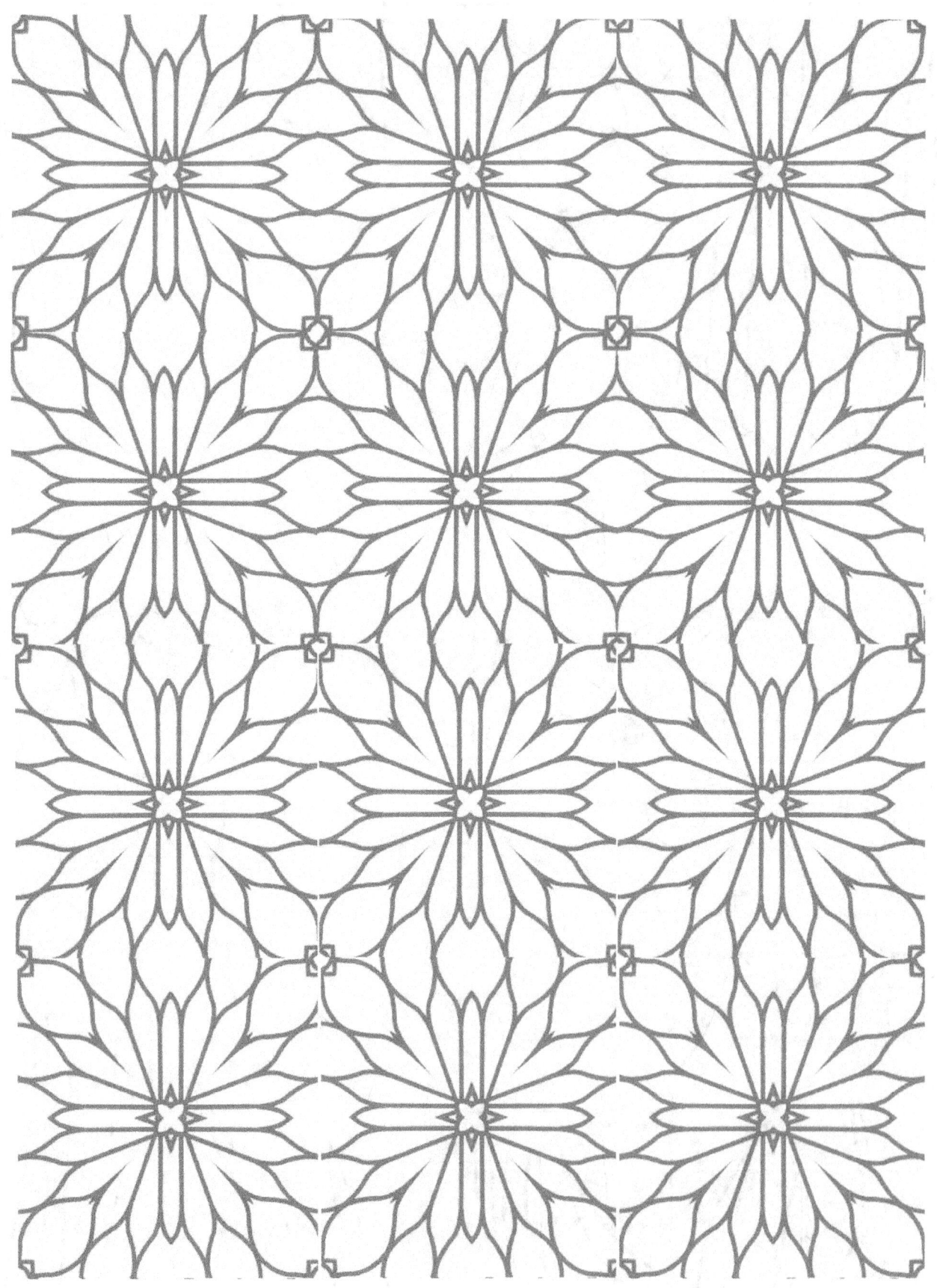

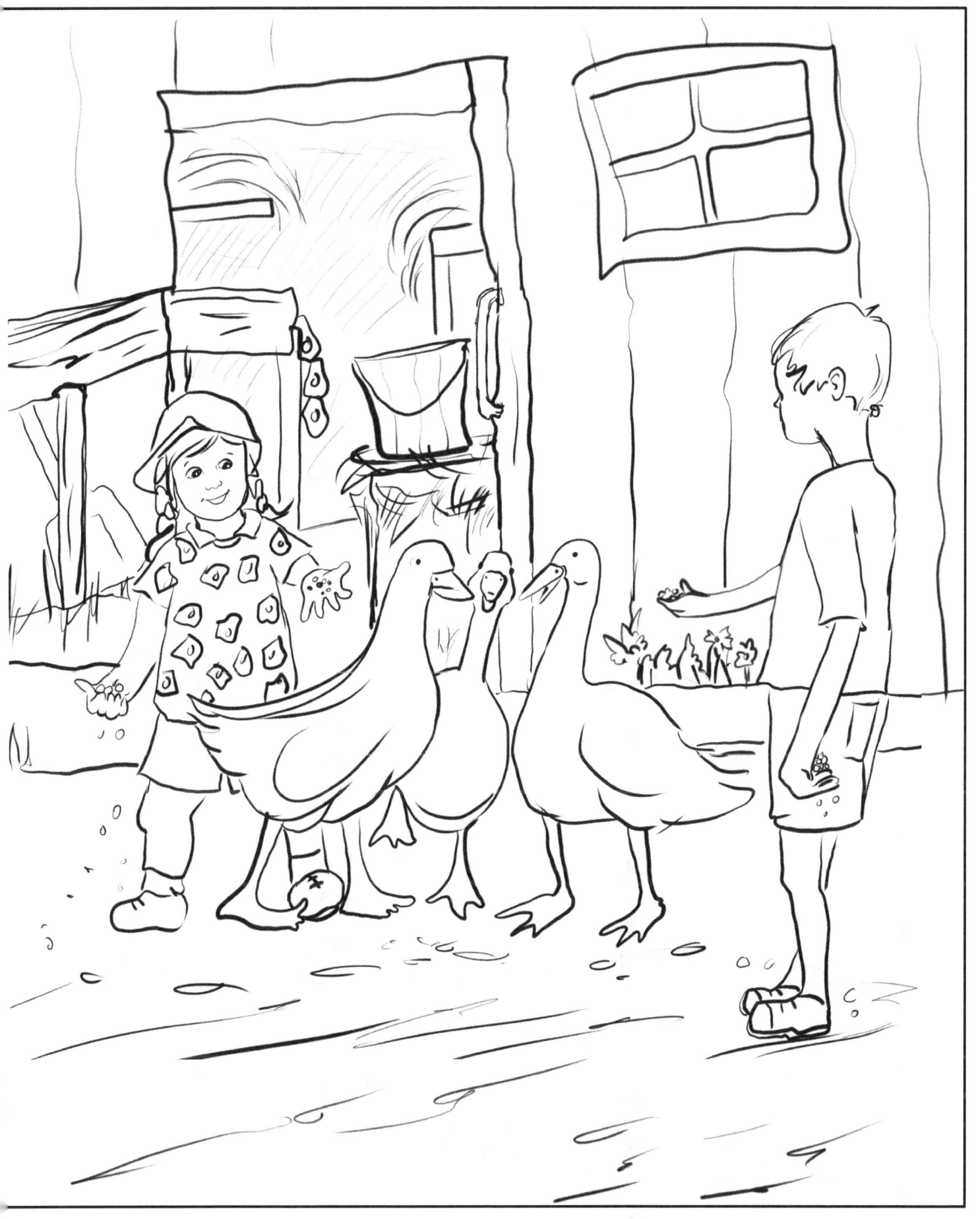

OH NO! Fox in the barnyard. Run away!

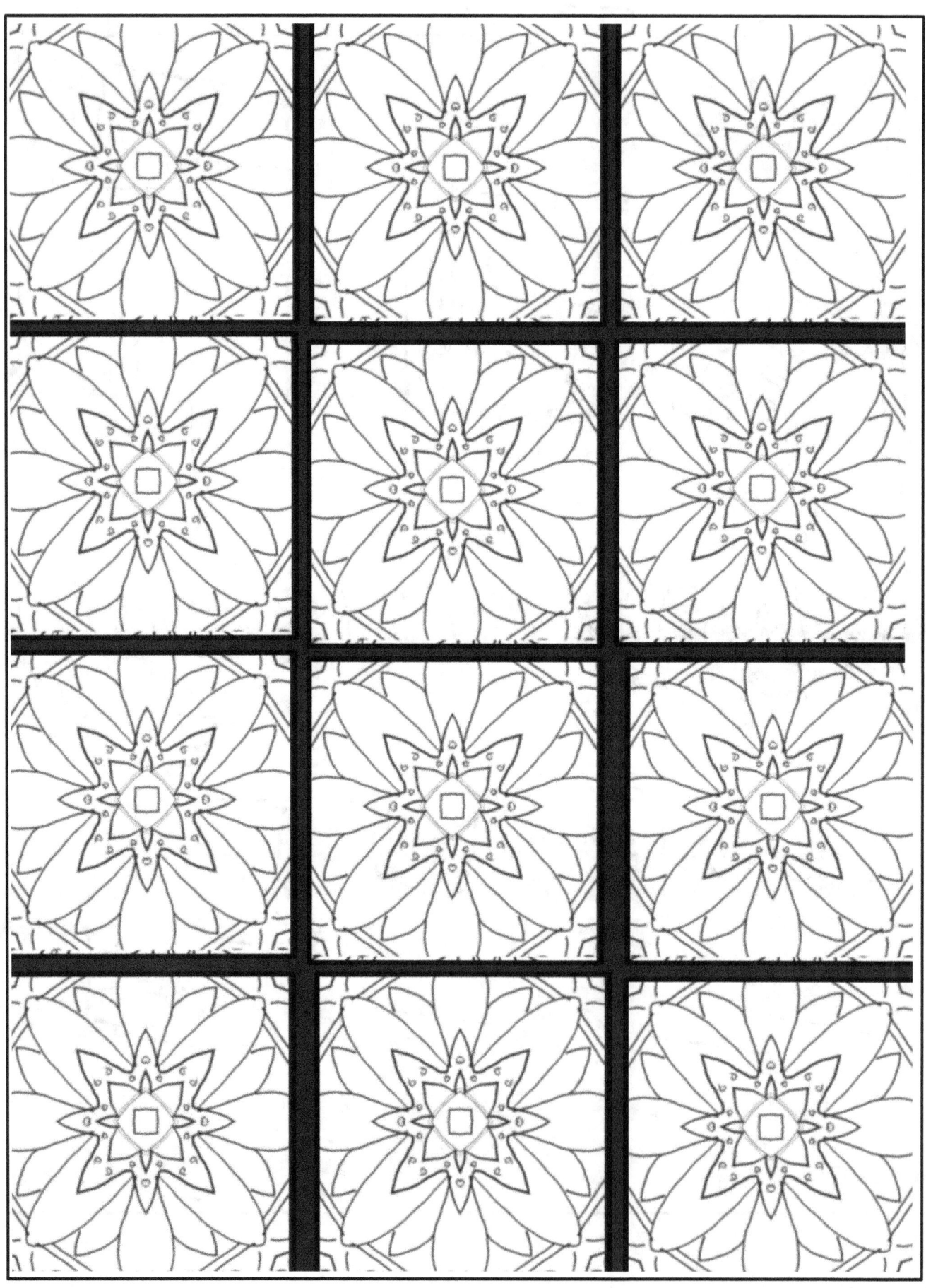

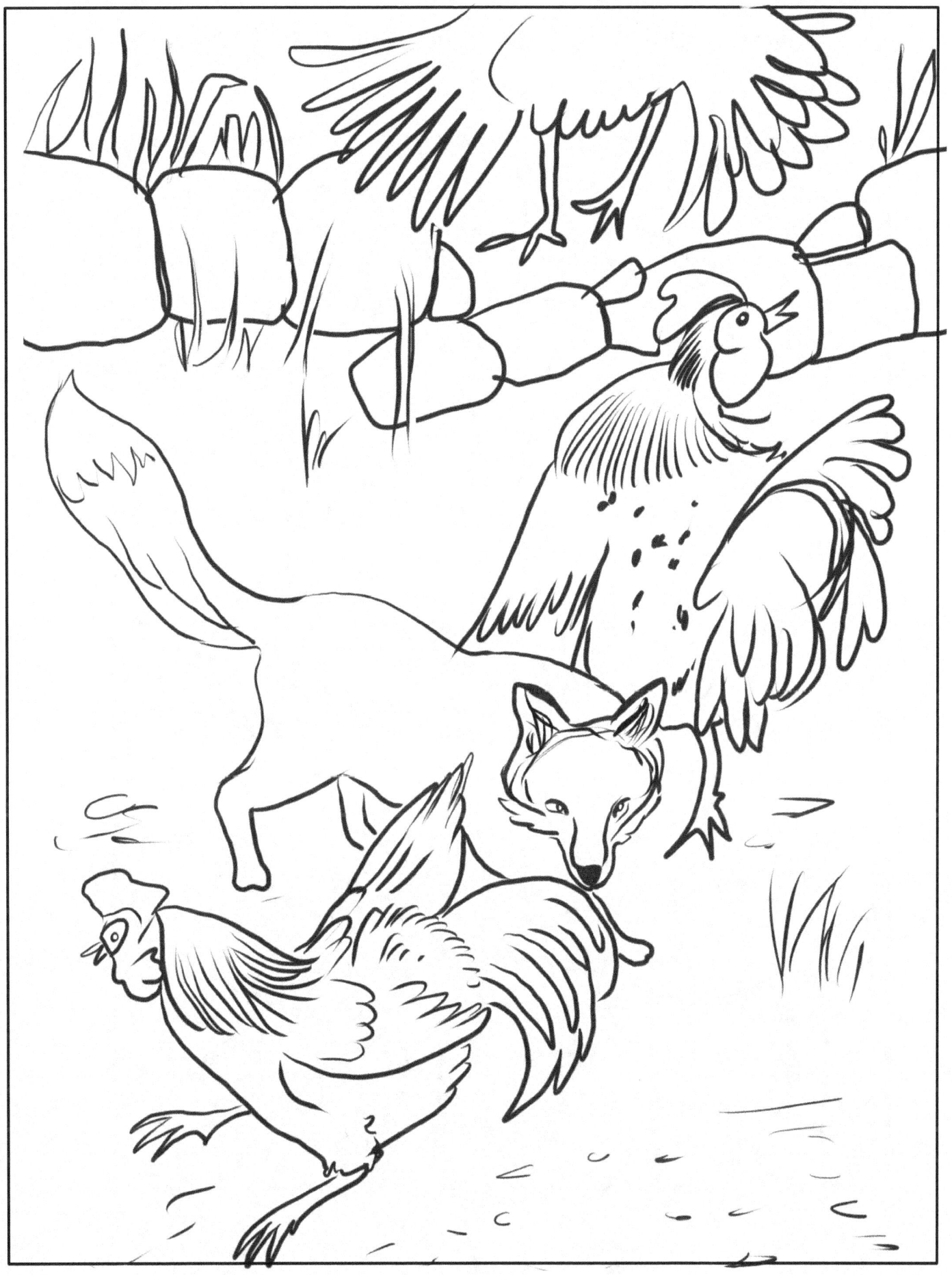

Take time to visit The Friendly Farm in Dublin.

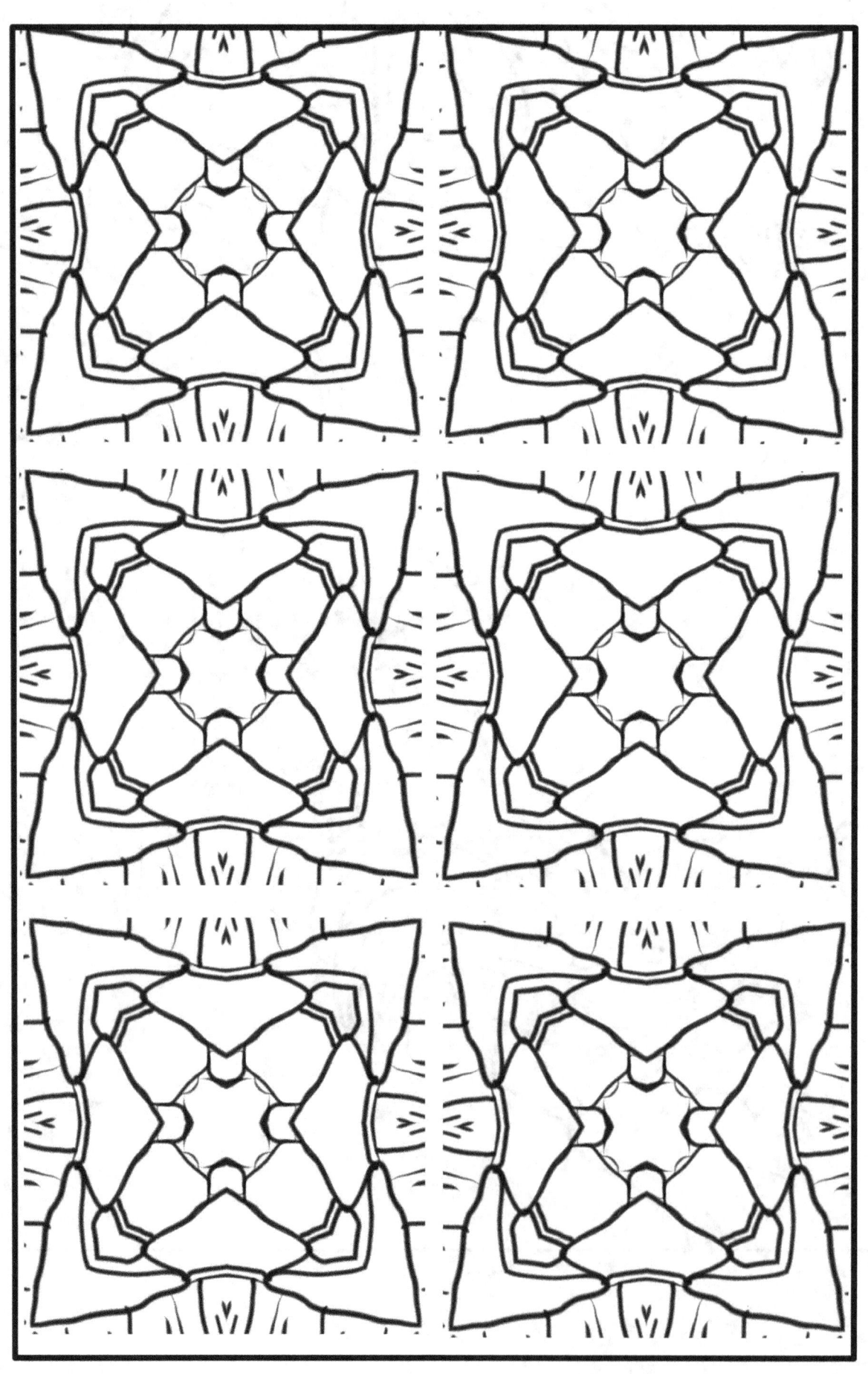

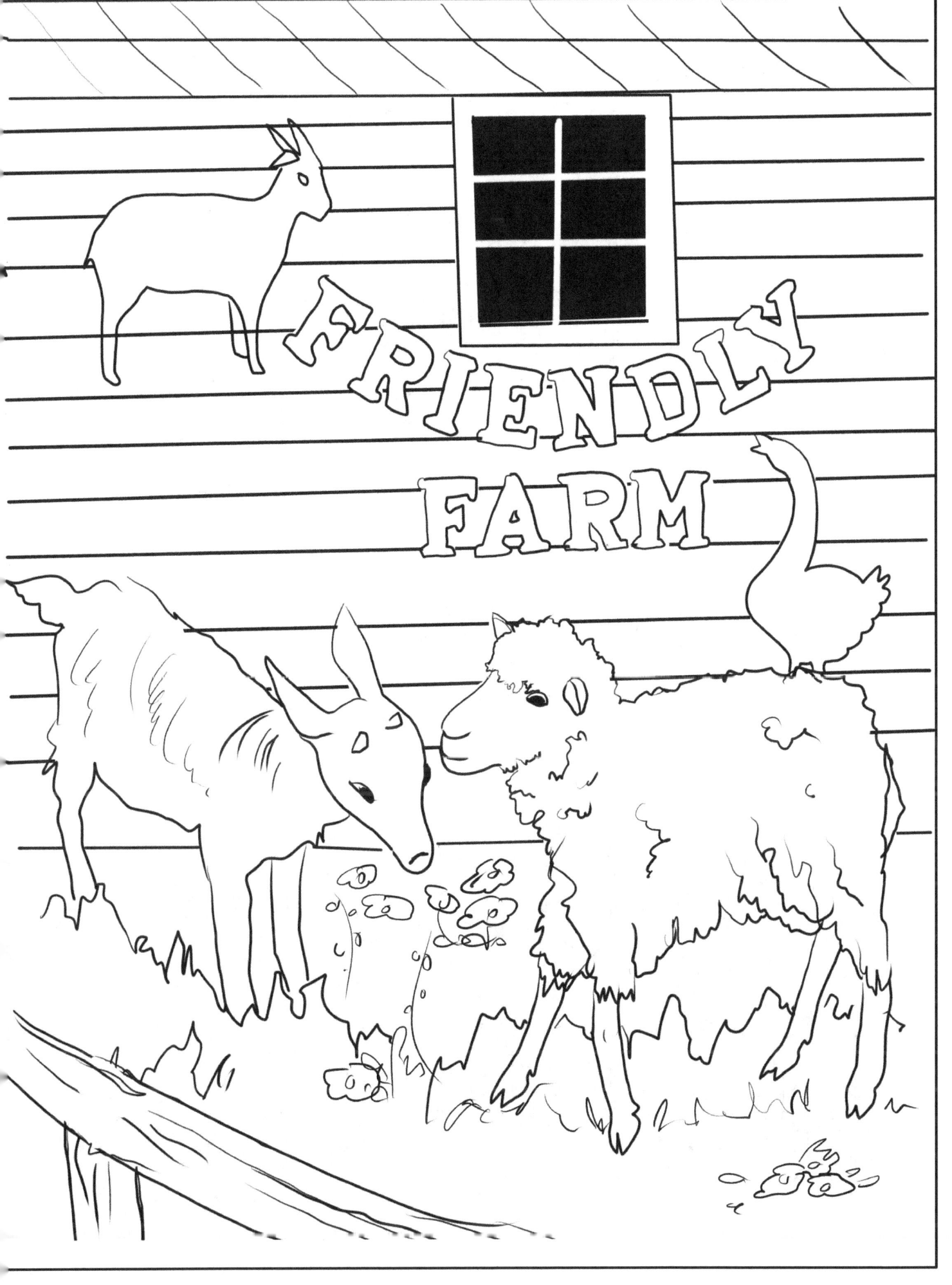

The historic Covered Bridge between Hancock, NH and Greenfield, NH

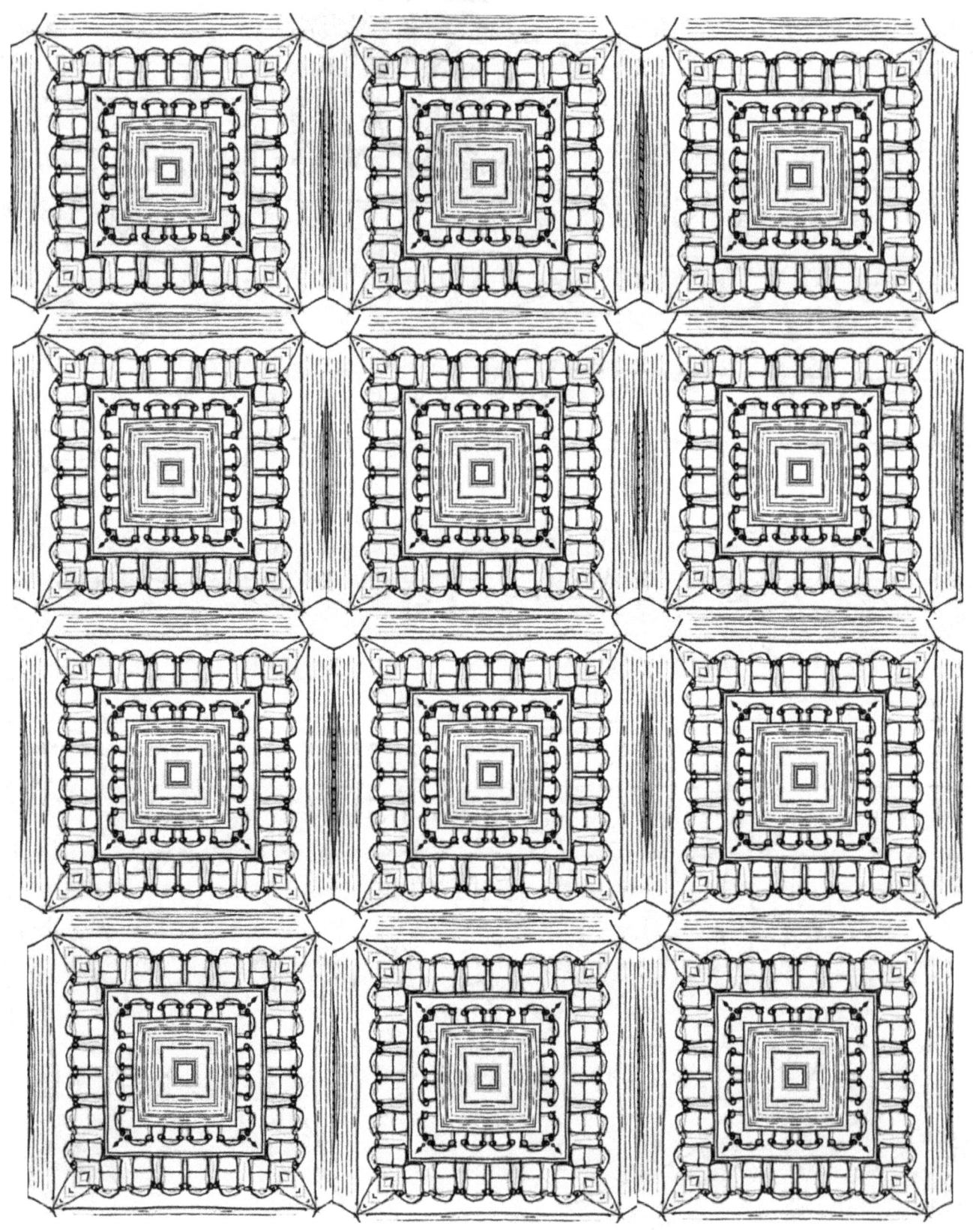

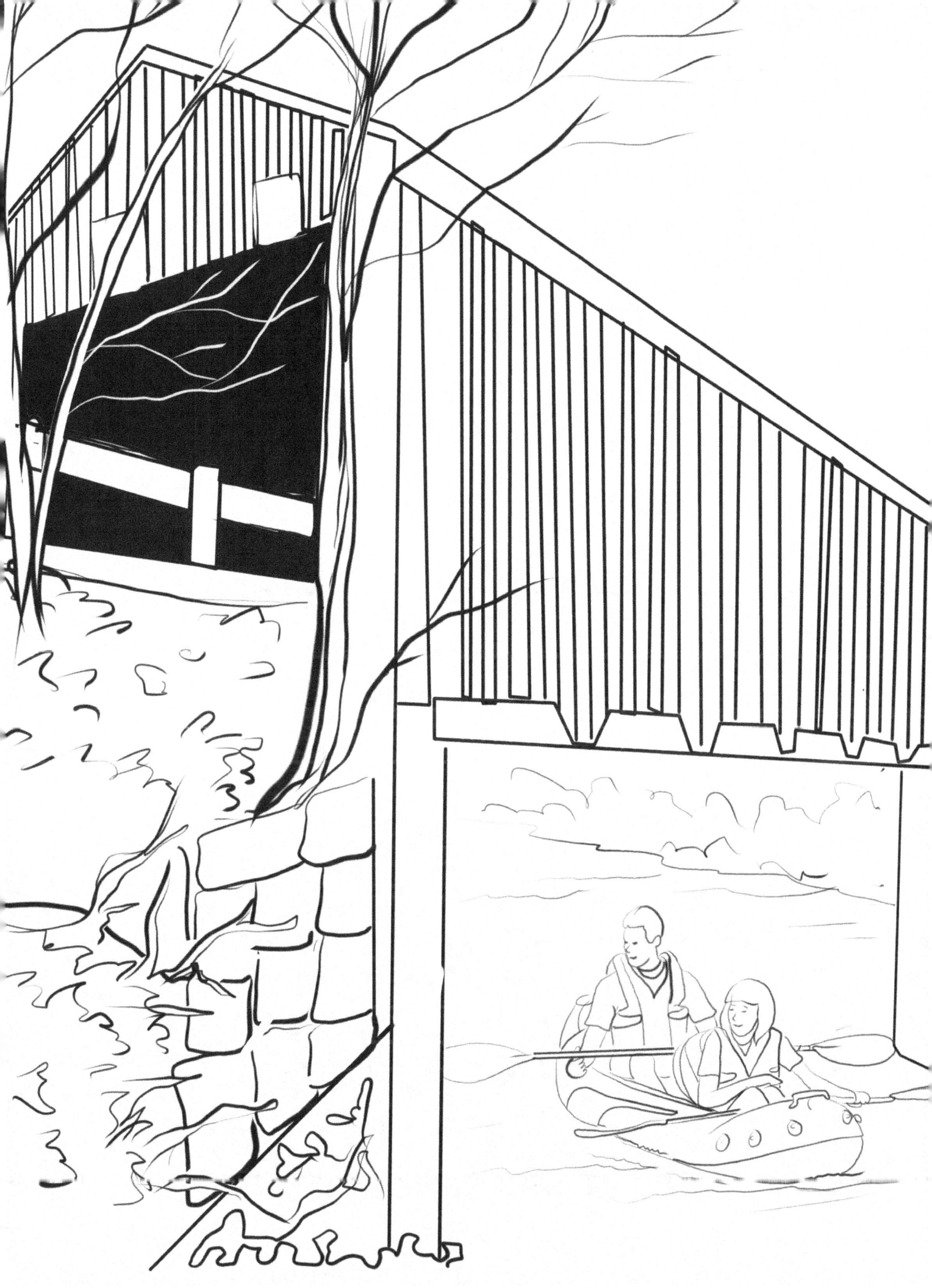

The Jesus Doll at Union Congregational Church in Peterborough, NH

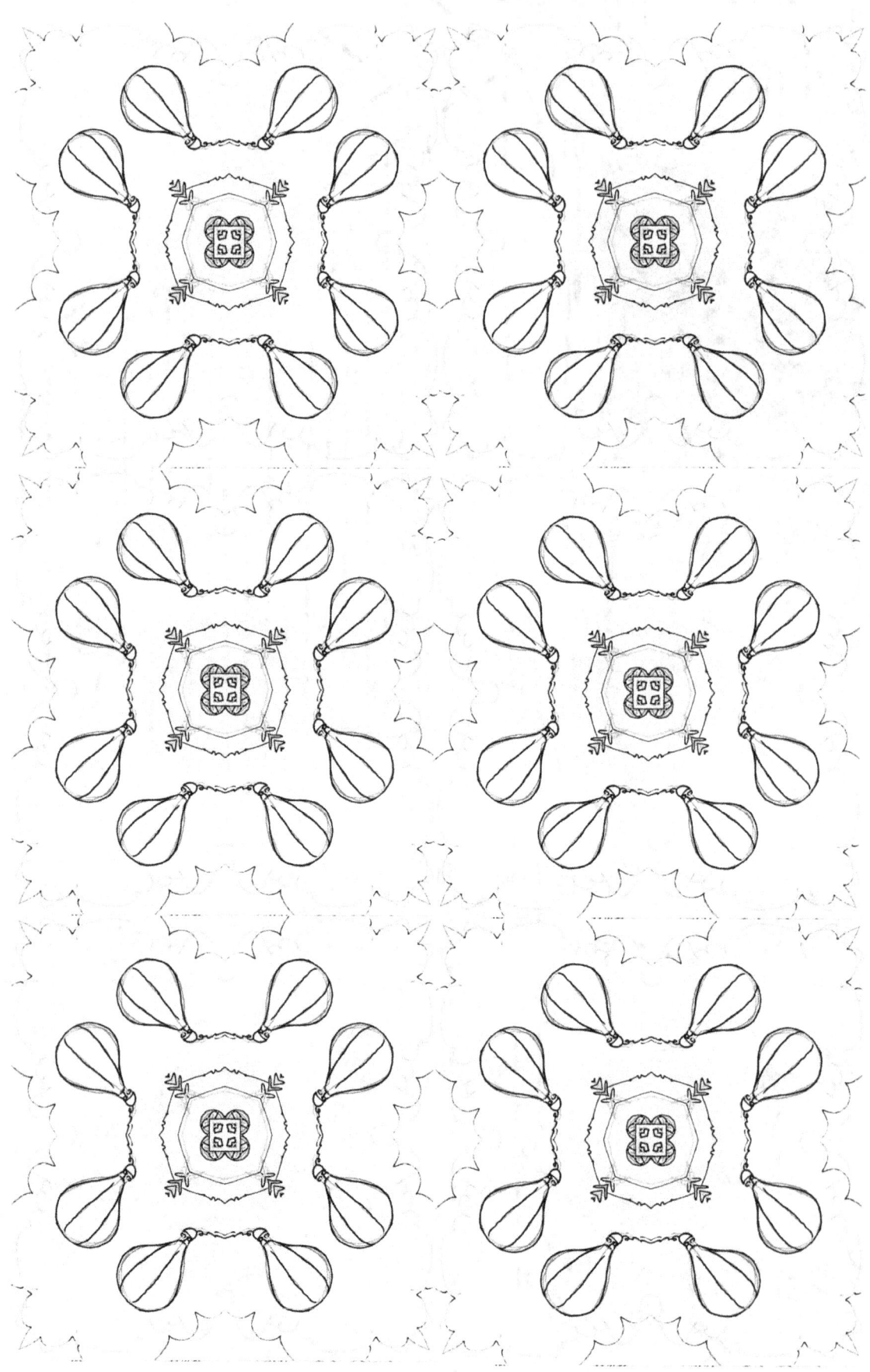

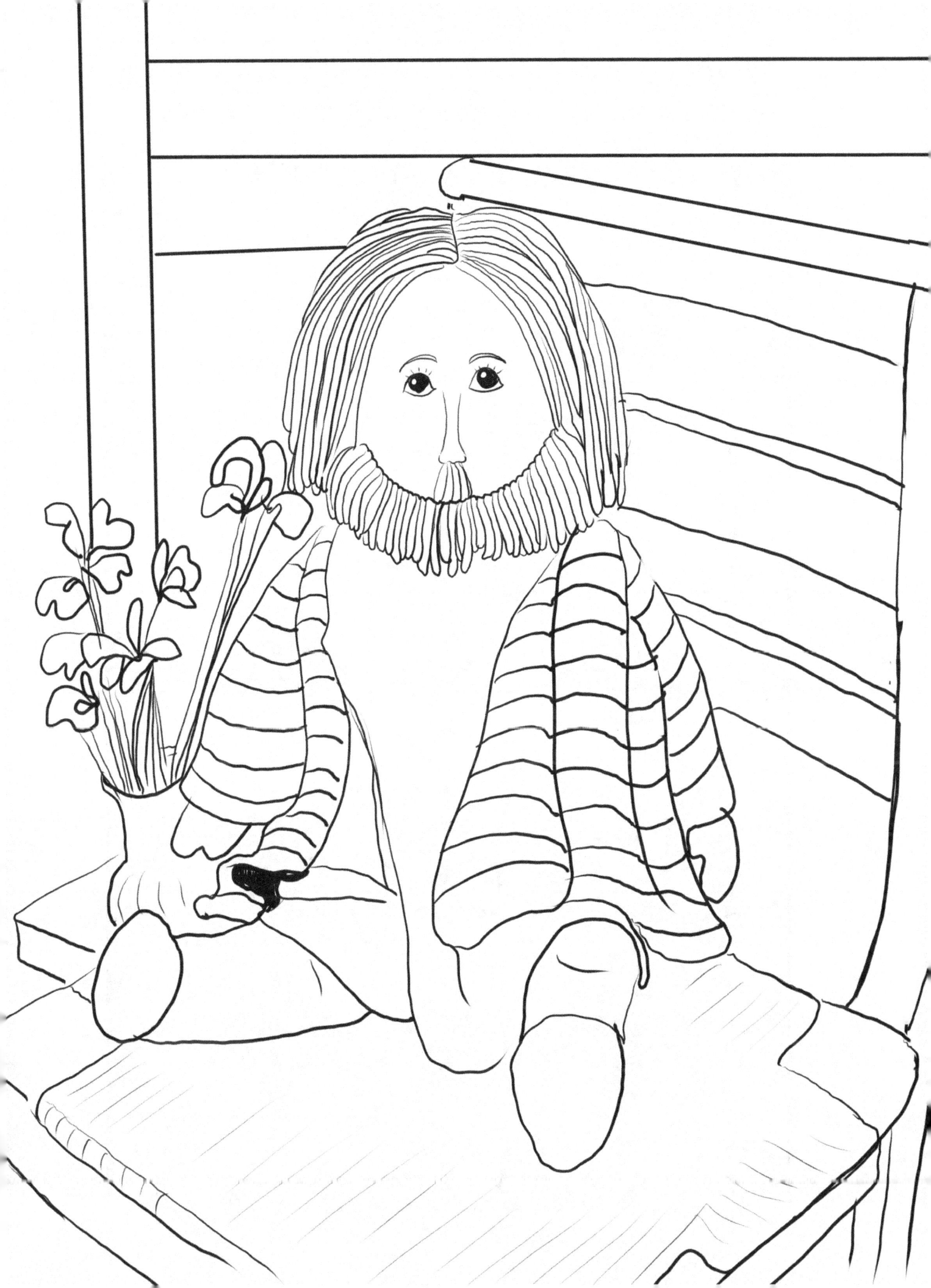

You may run into any one of these creatures in the many forests and even backyards of NH.

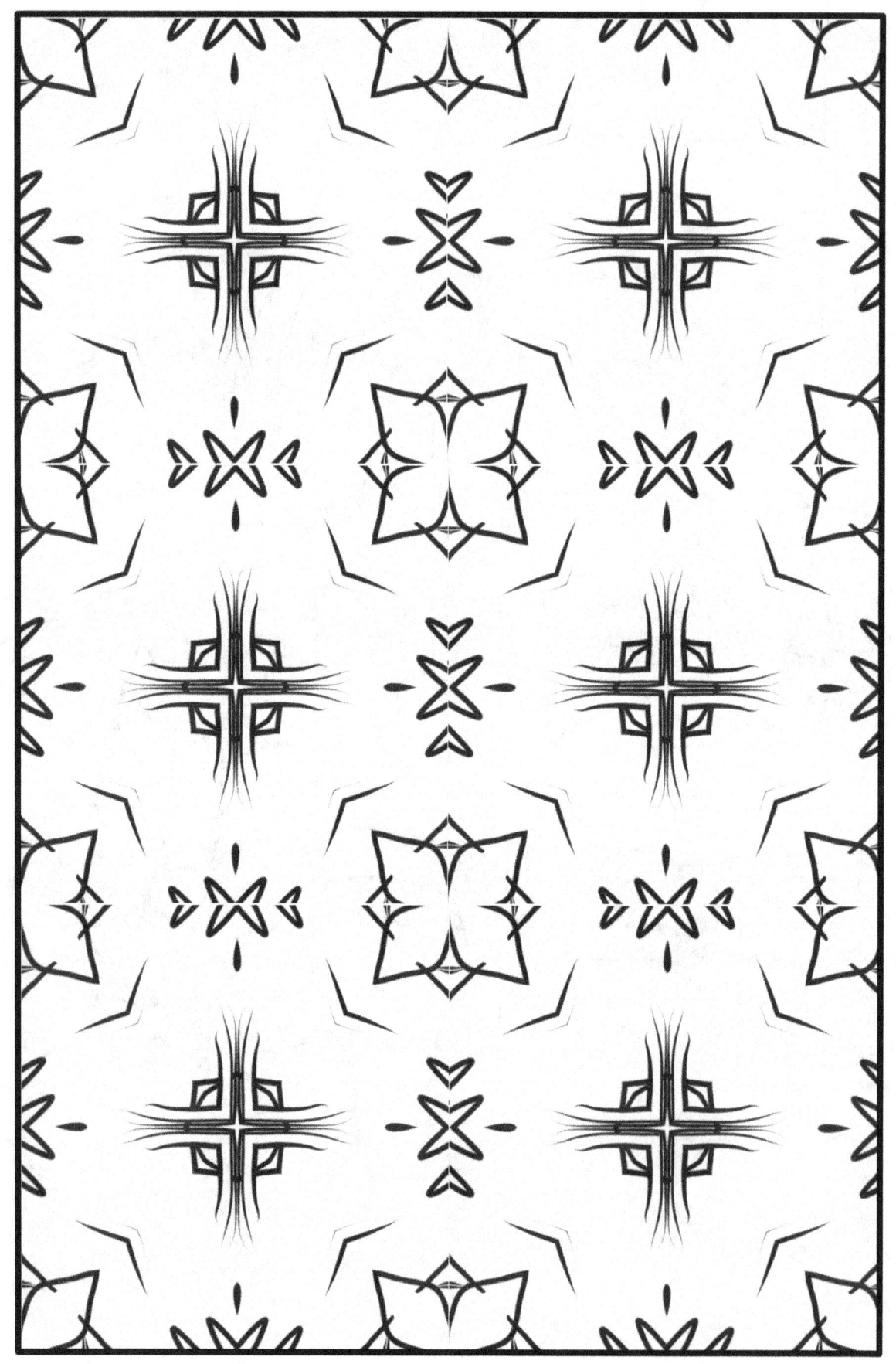

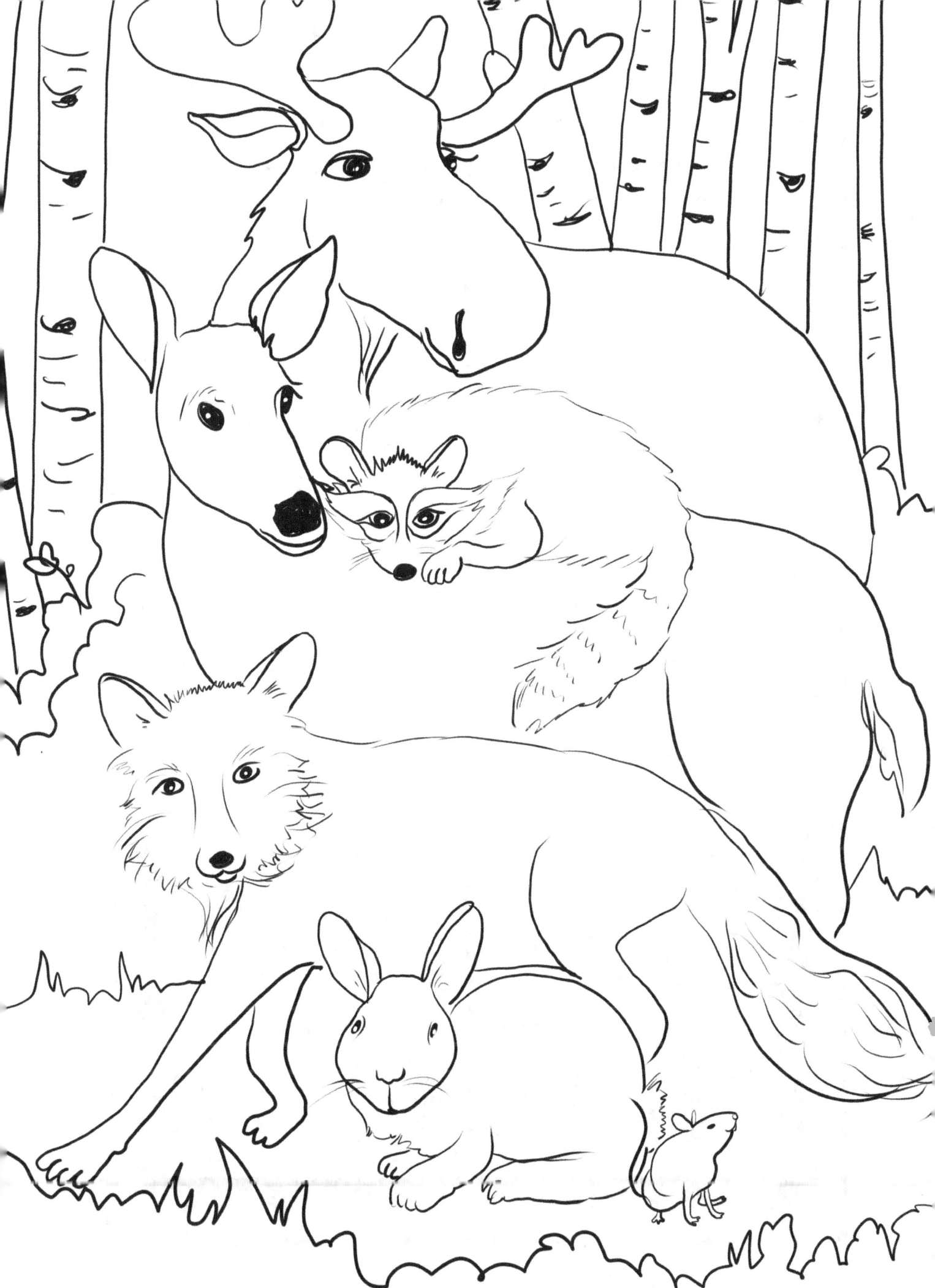

Mt. Monadnock is the most climbed mountain in the United States.

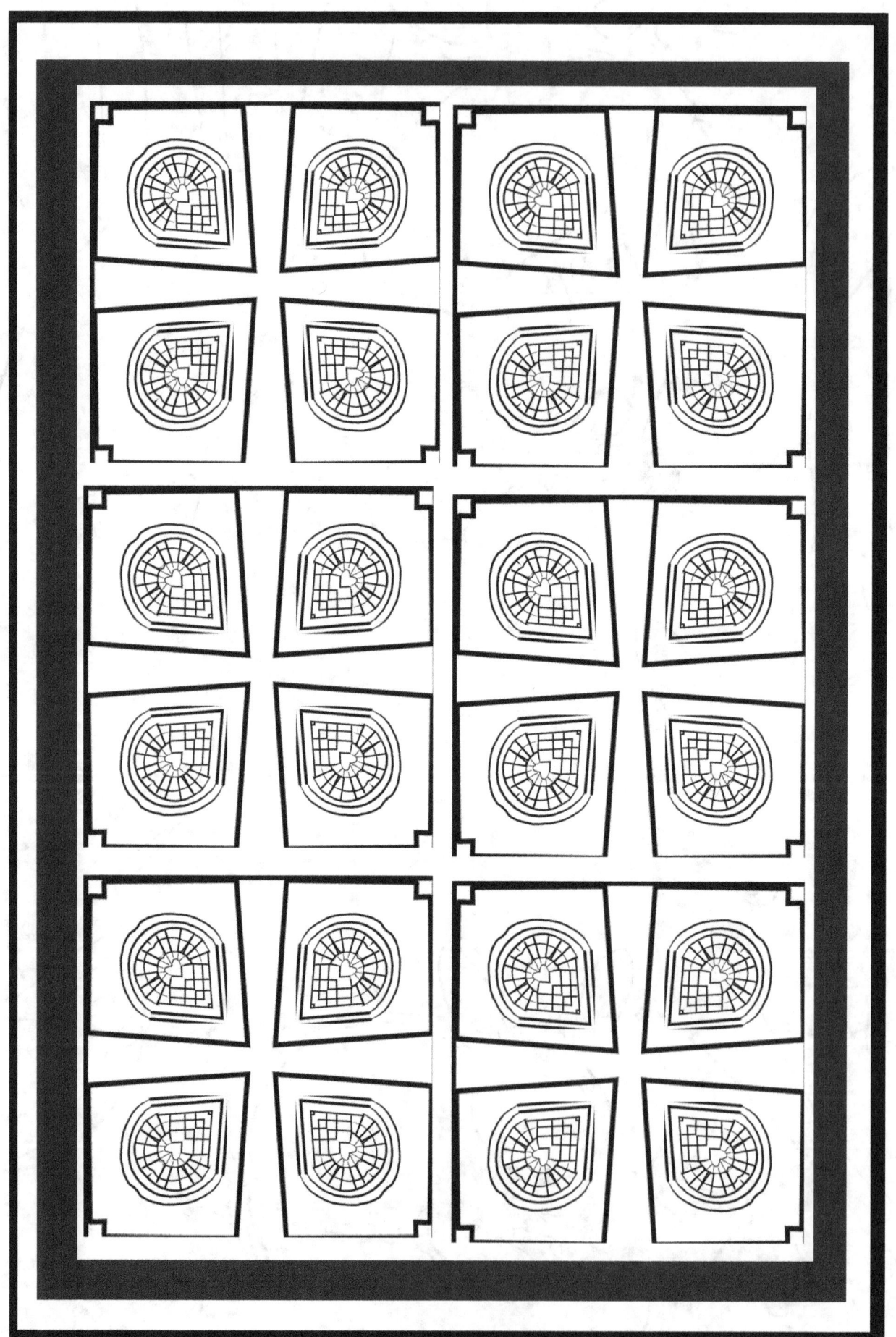

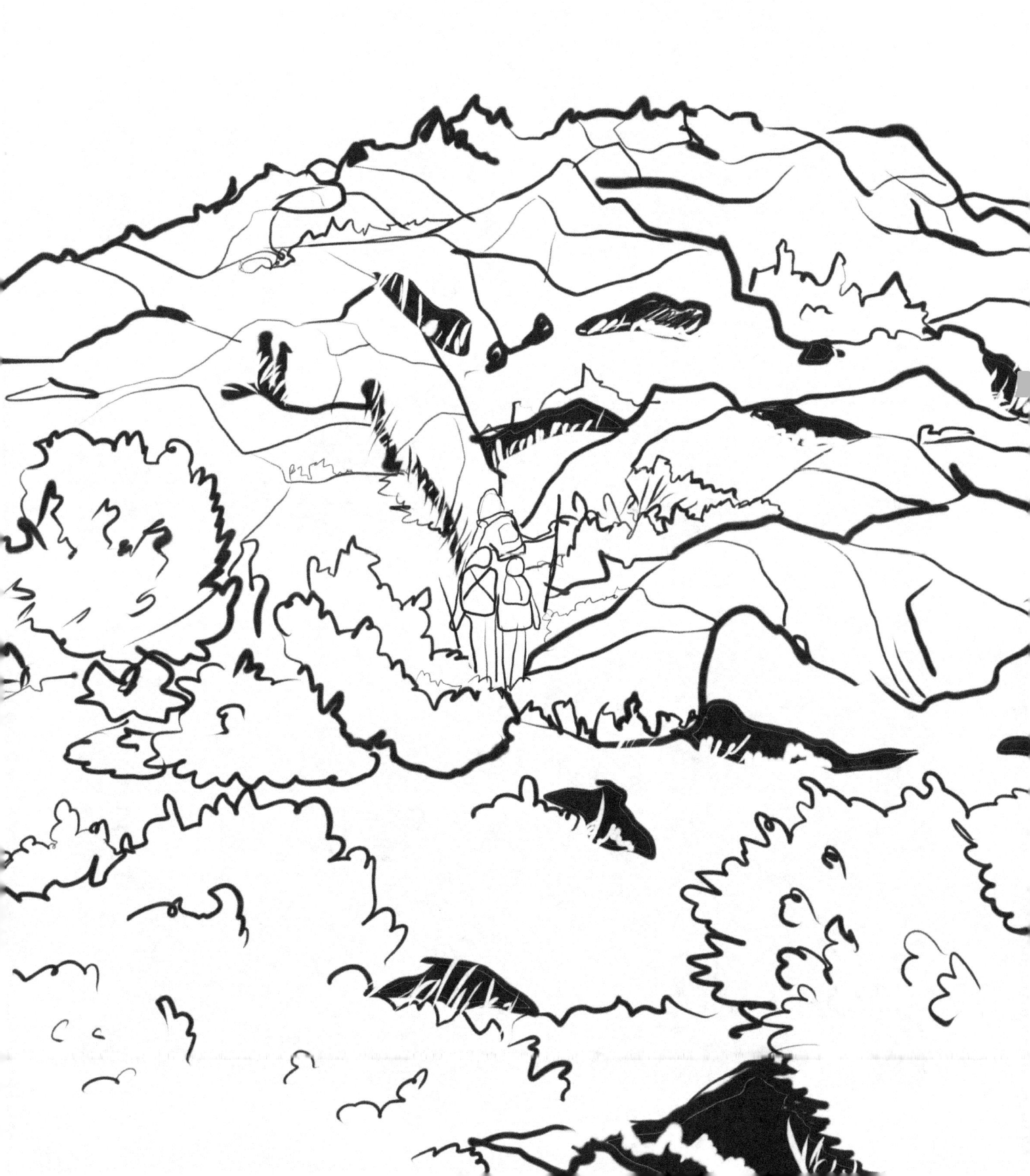

The Apple Orchard on Norway Hill in Hancock, NH.

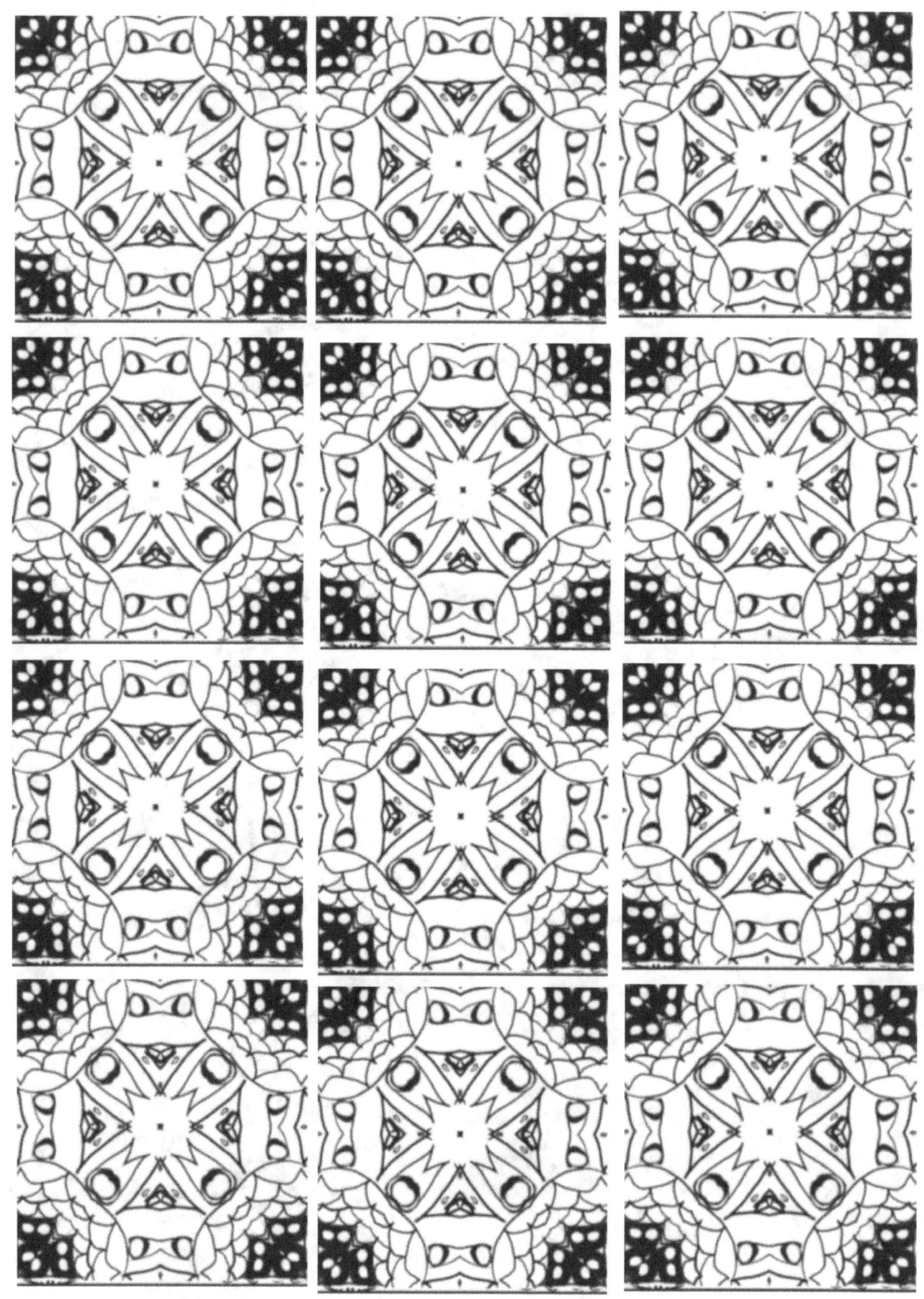

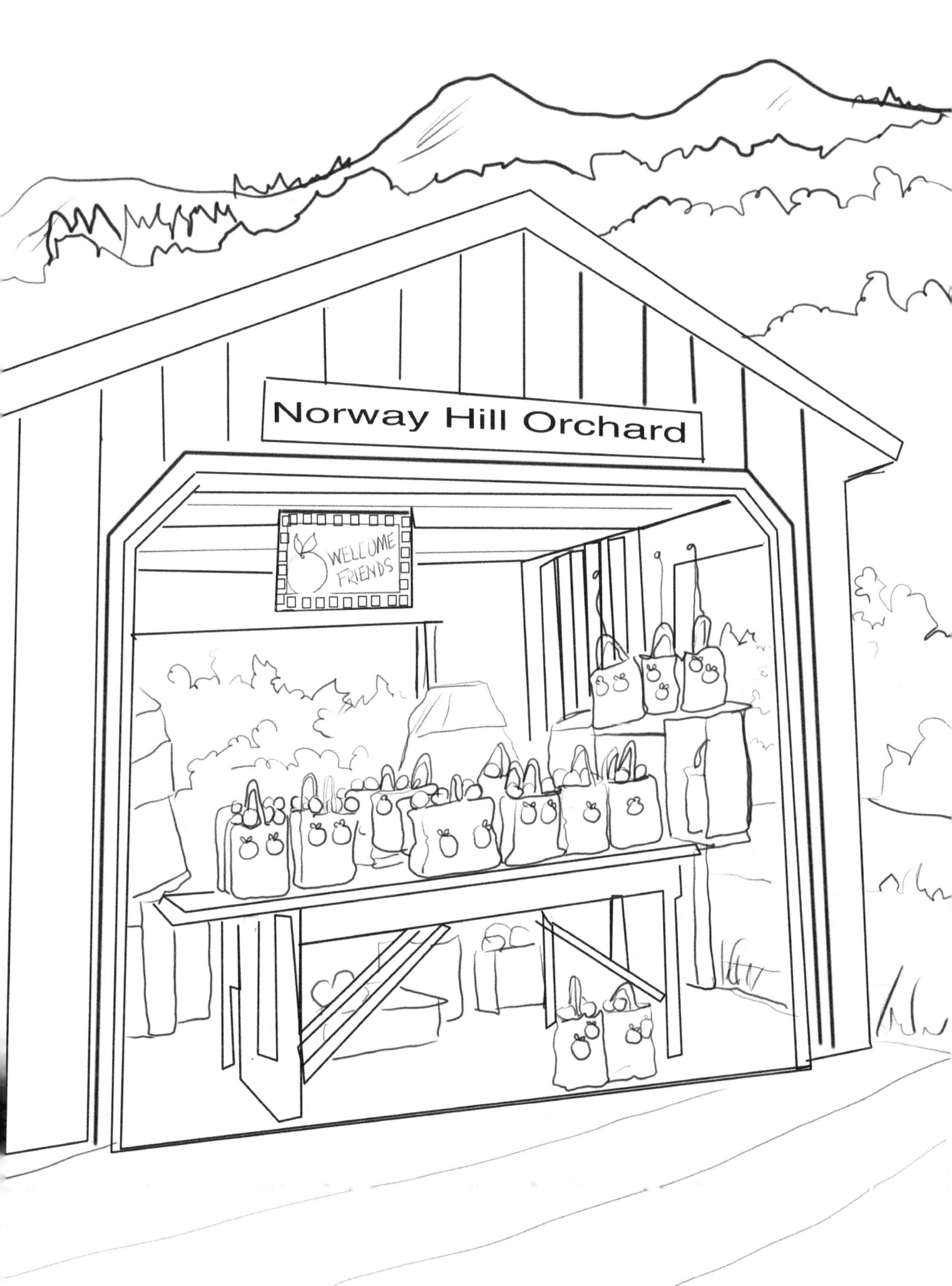

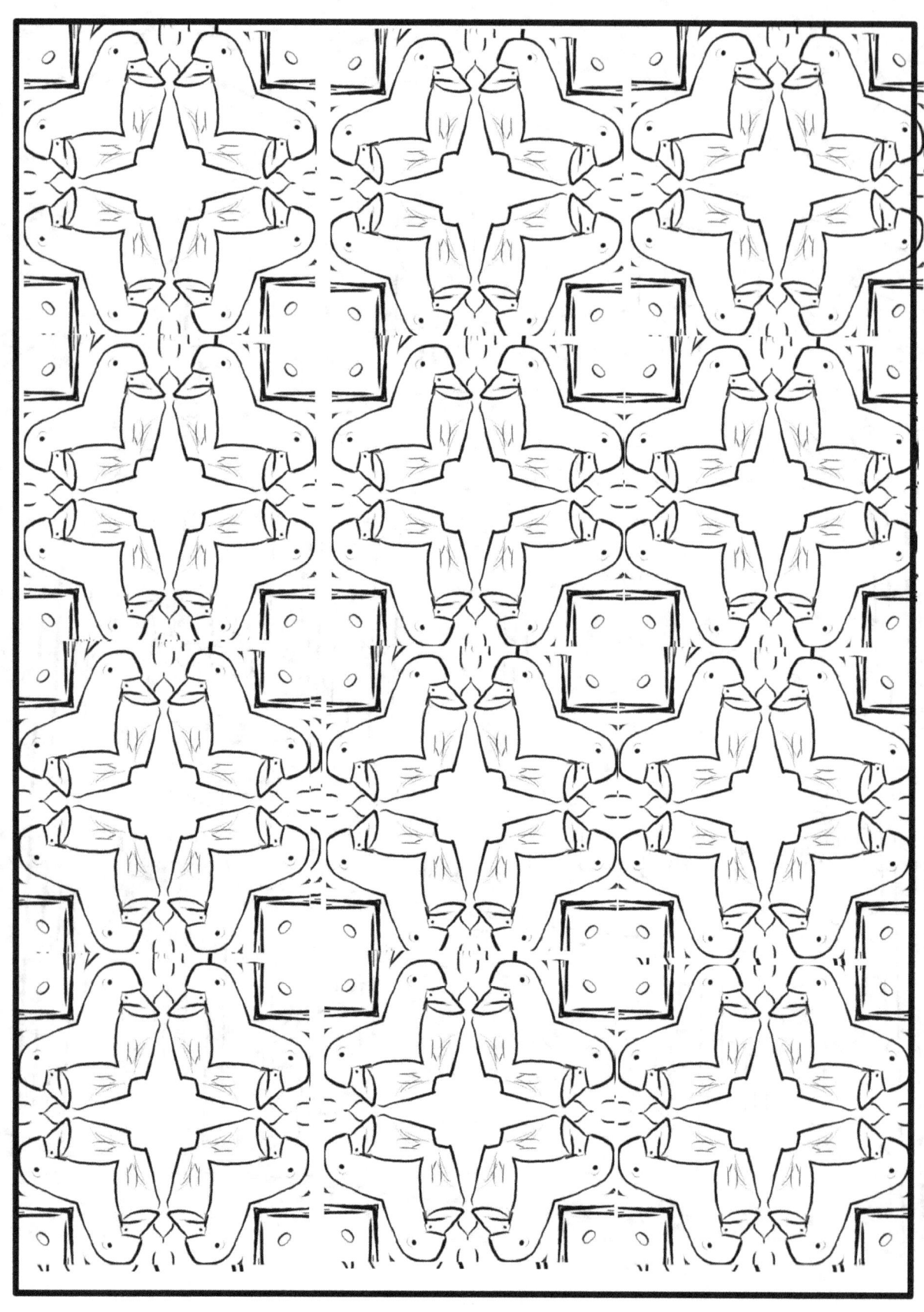

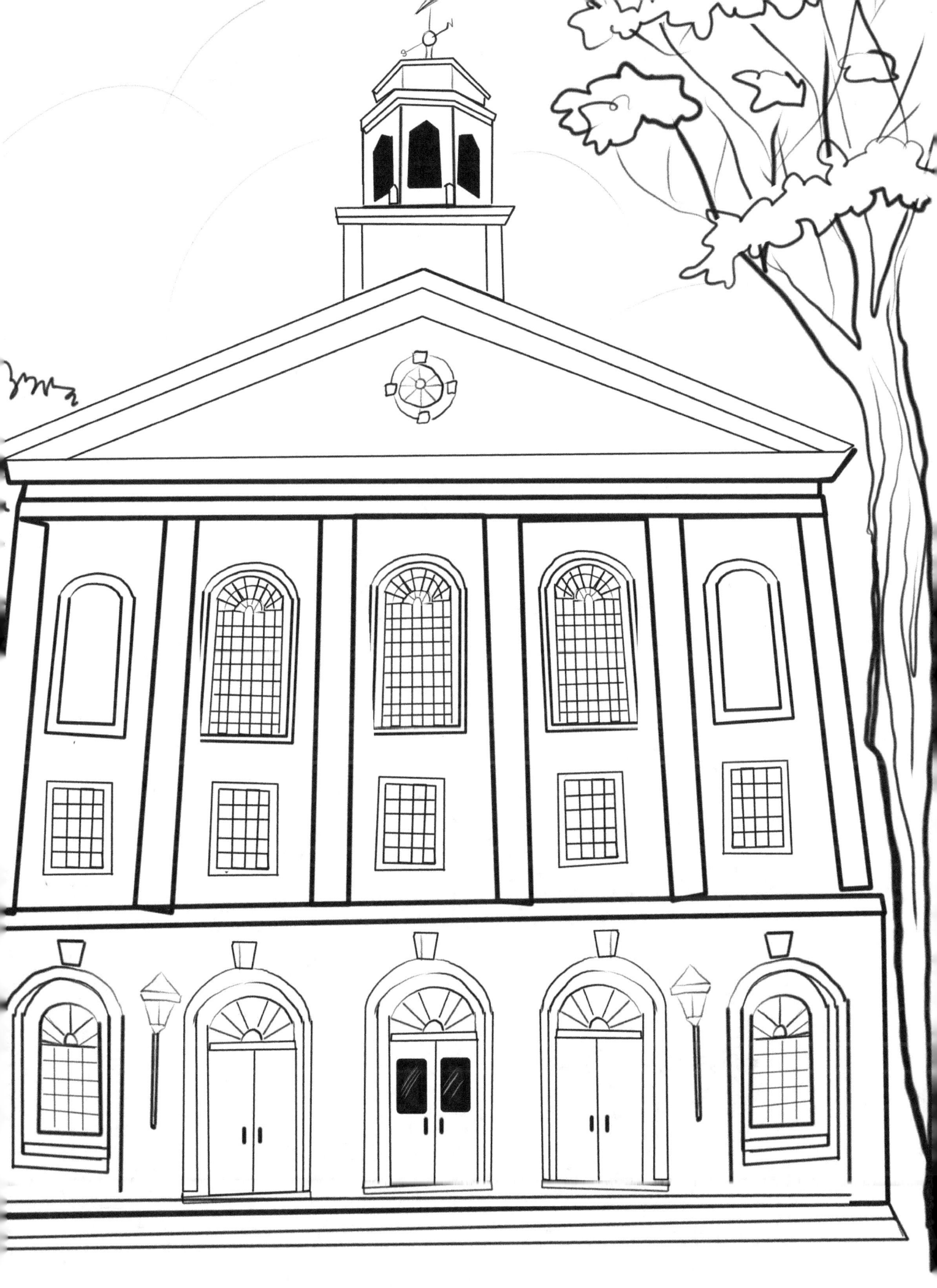

For many years a Pumpkin Festival was held in Keene.

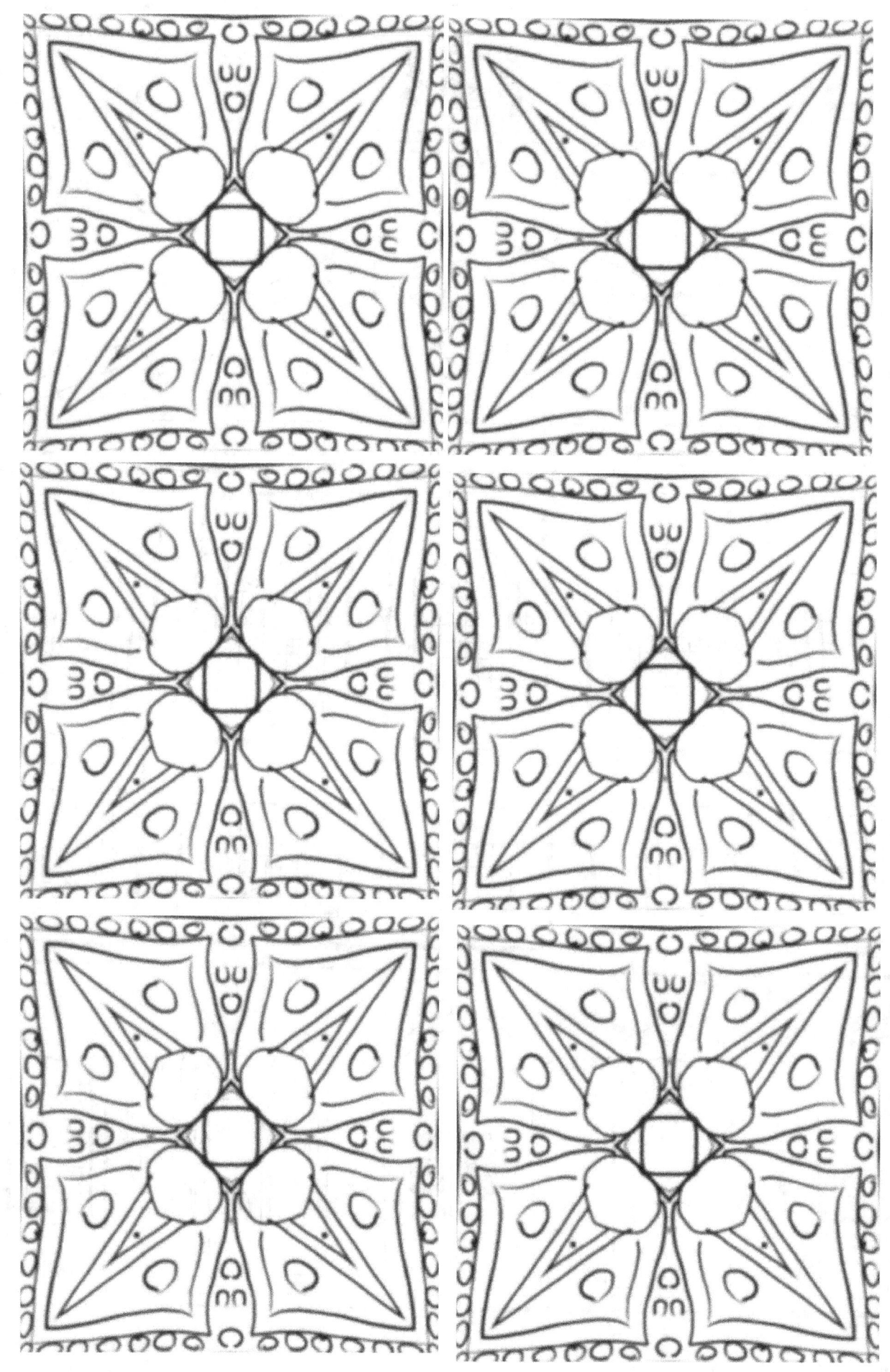

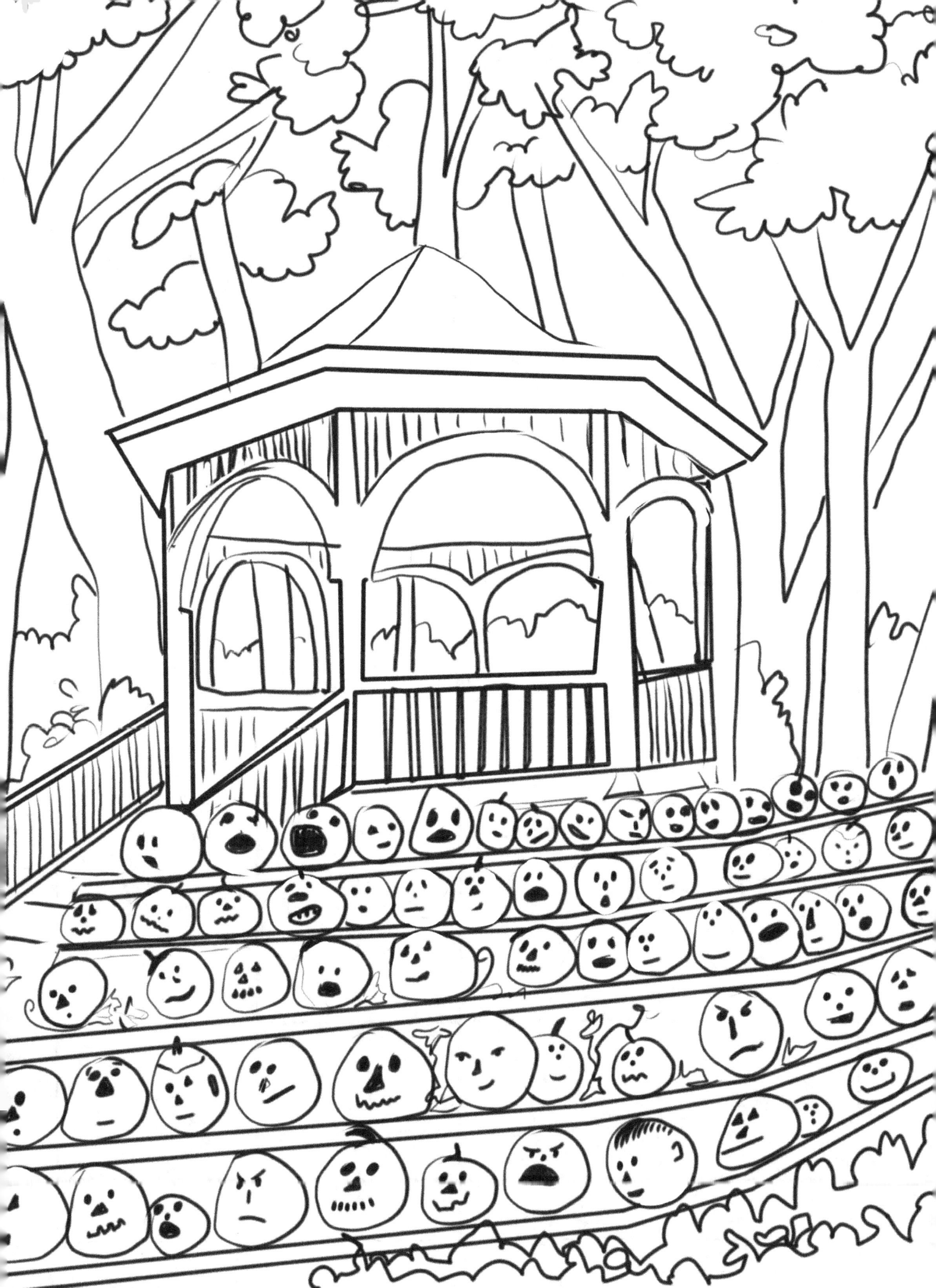

The Monadnock Area holds miles of stone walls.

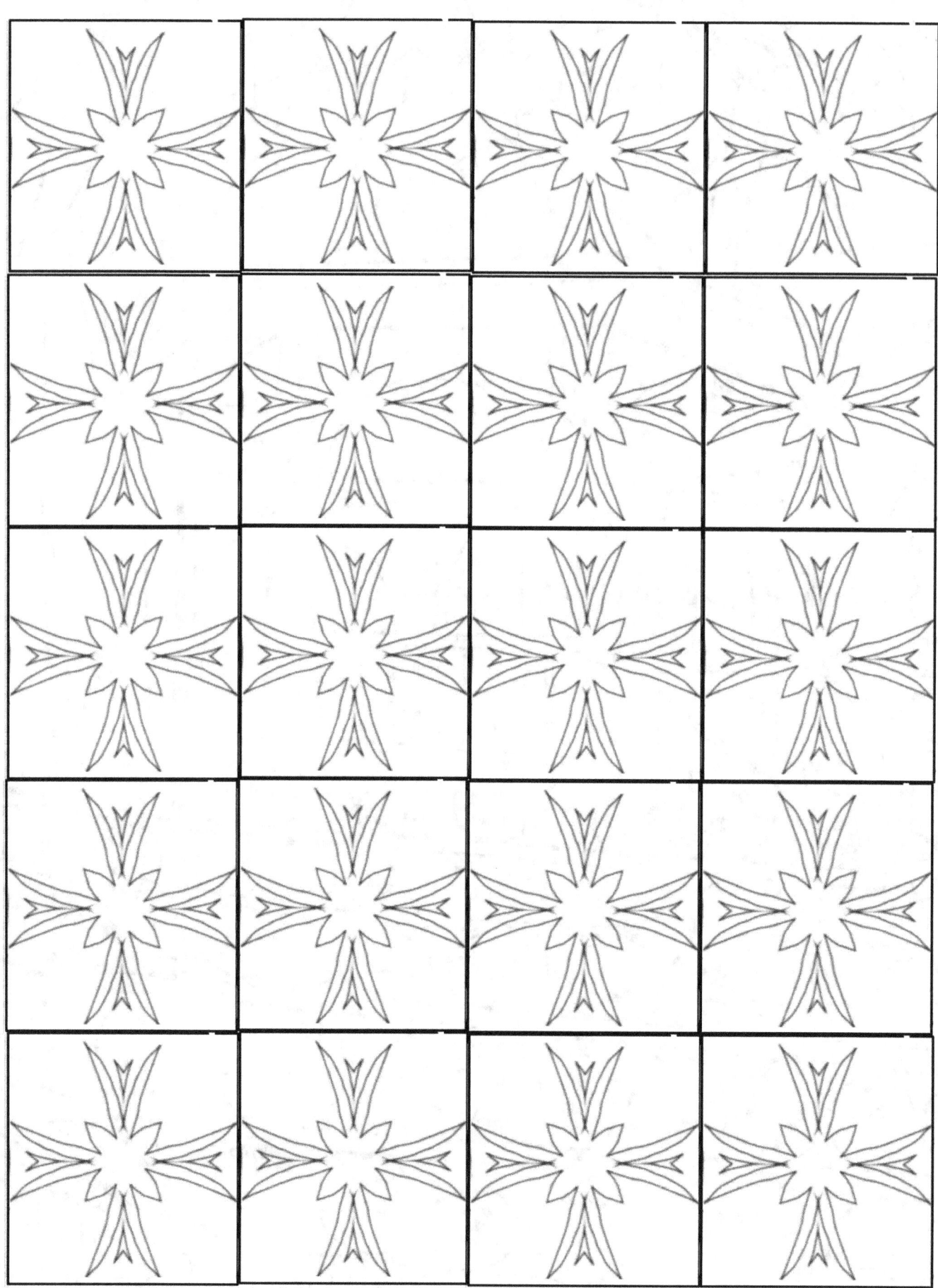

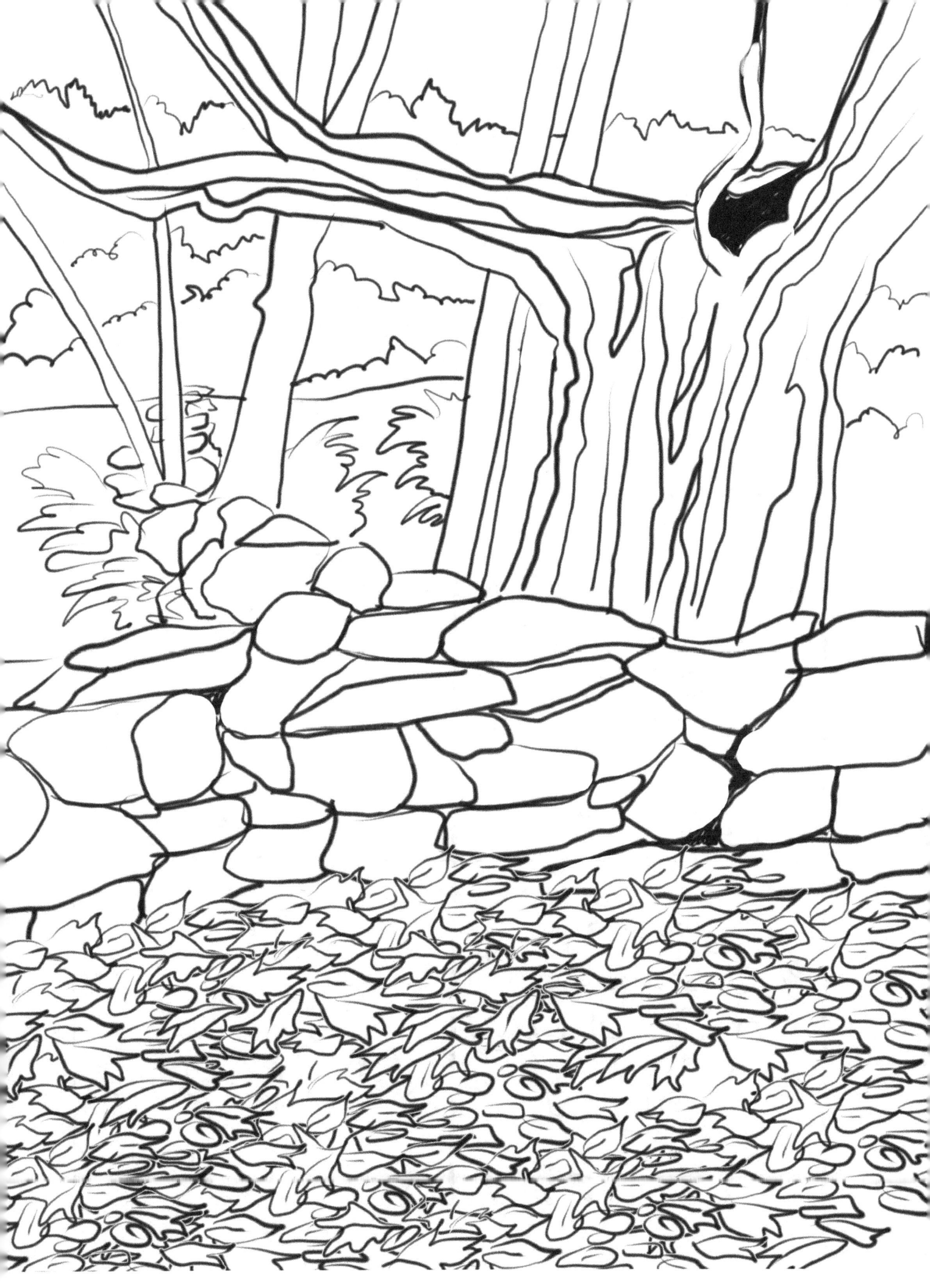

Come see the scarecrows in Jaffrey, NH every fall.

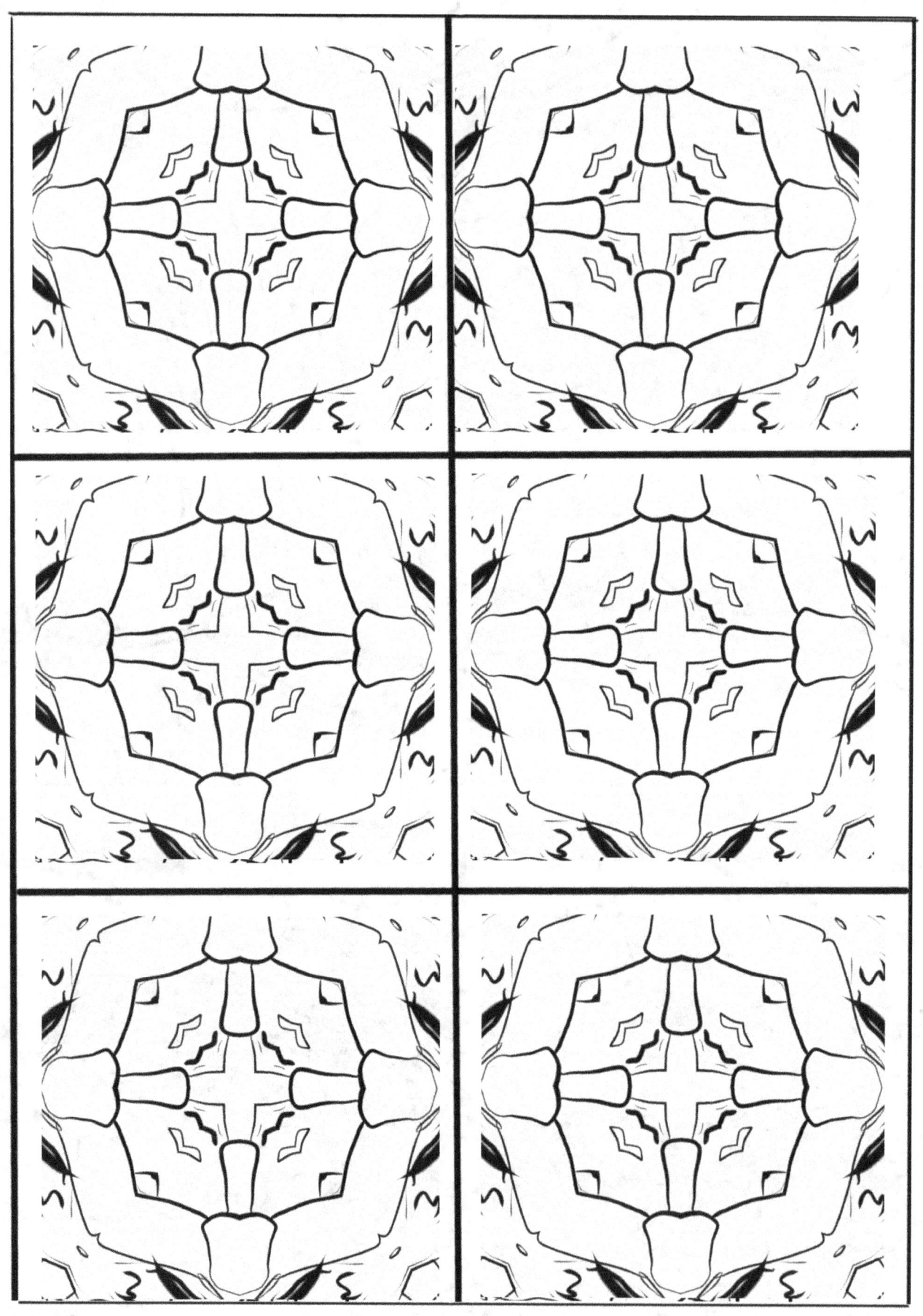

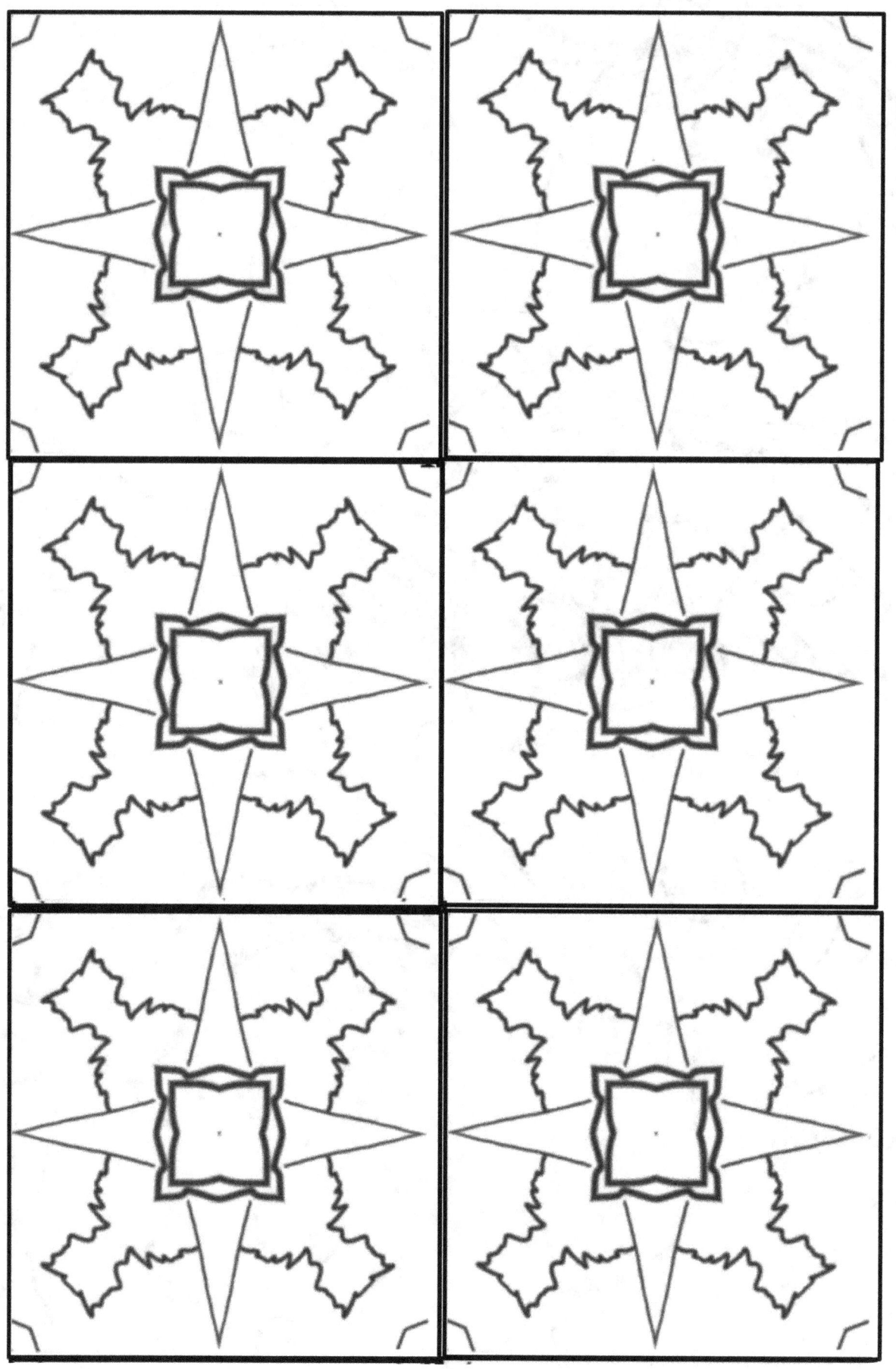

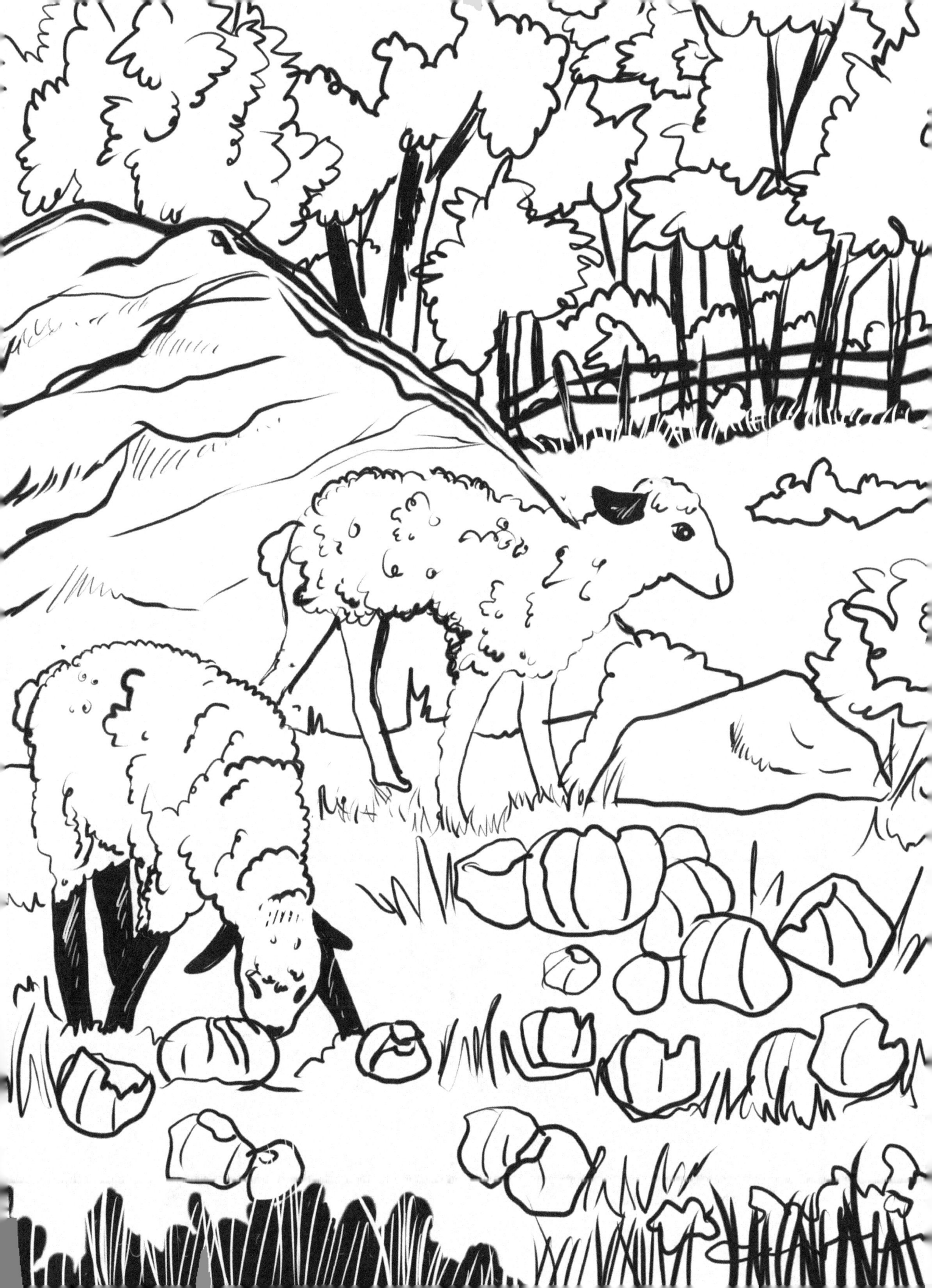

Wild turkeys are abundant in the Monadnocks.

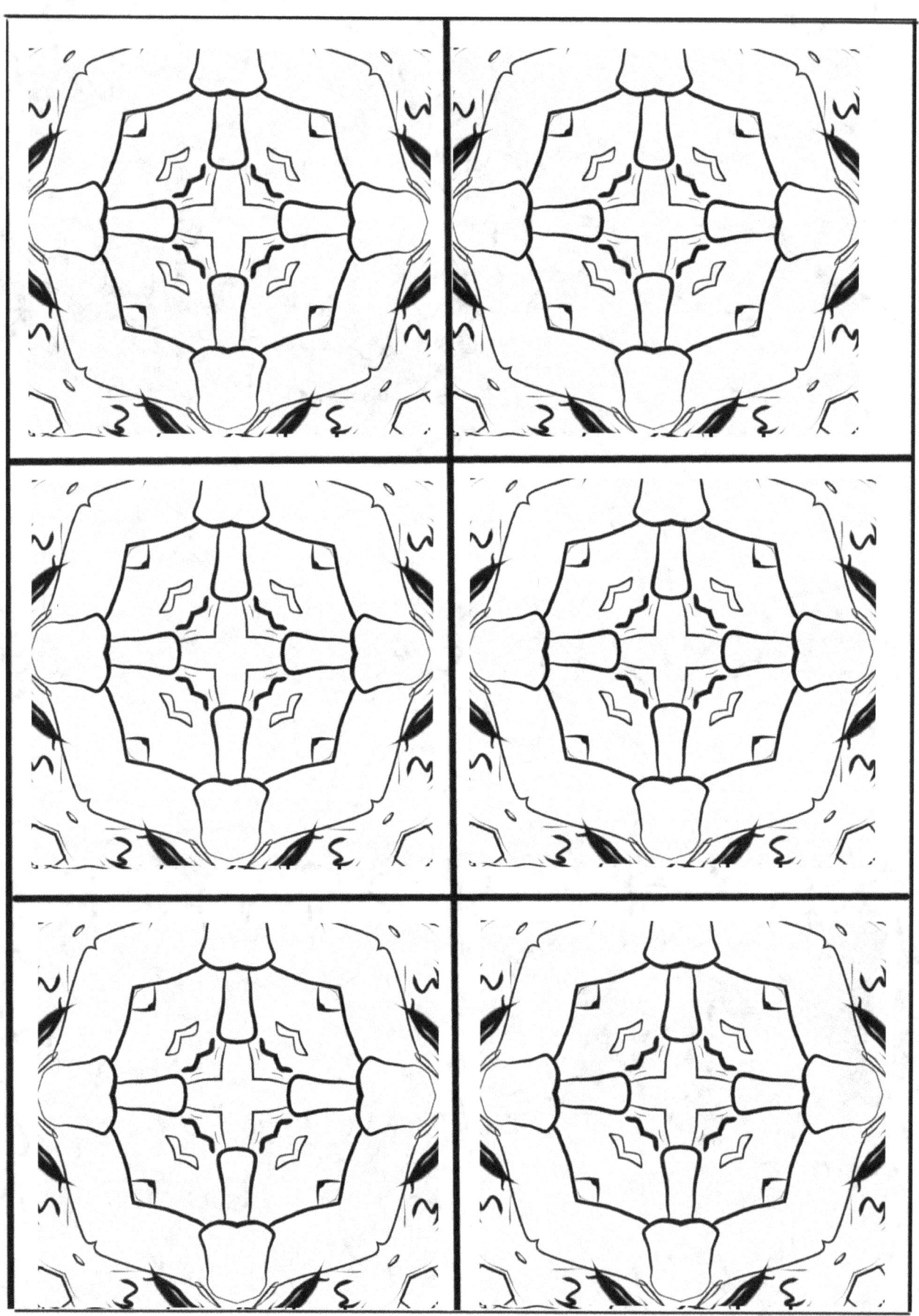

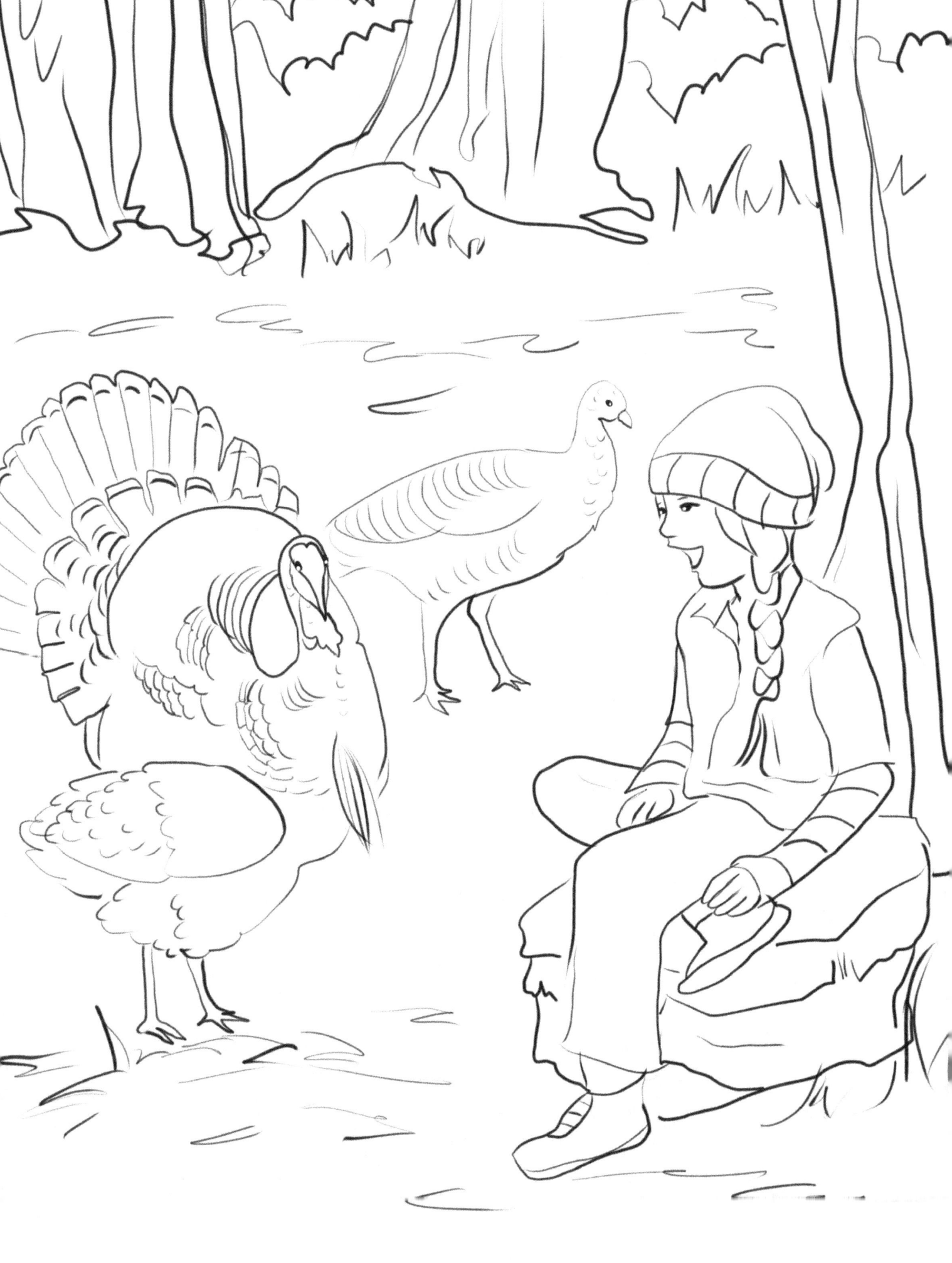

Volunteers pack weekend nourishment for area children in need as part of the End 68 Hours program.

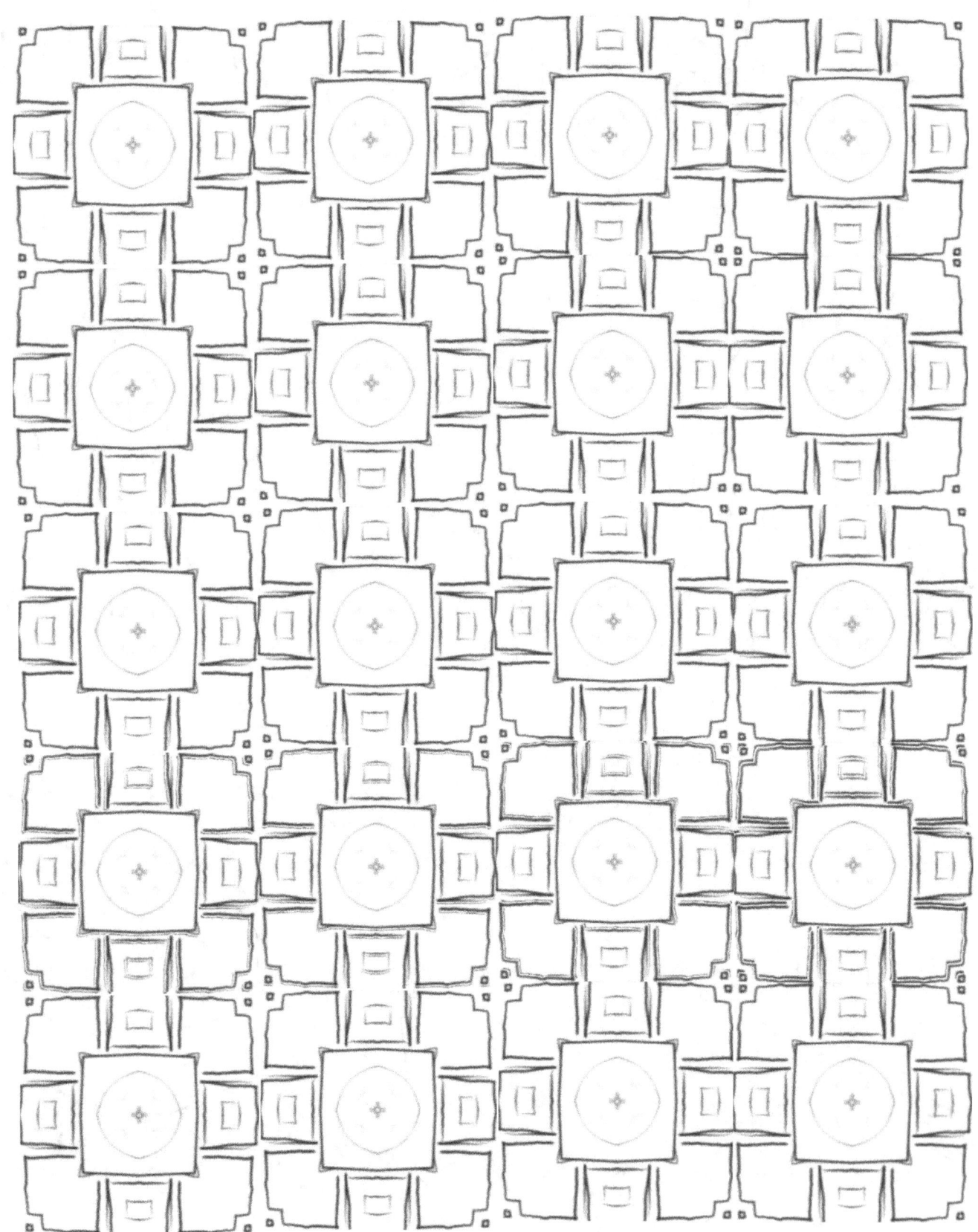

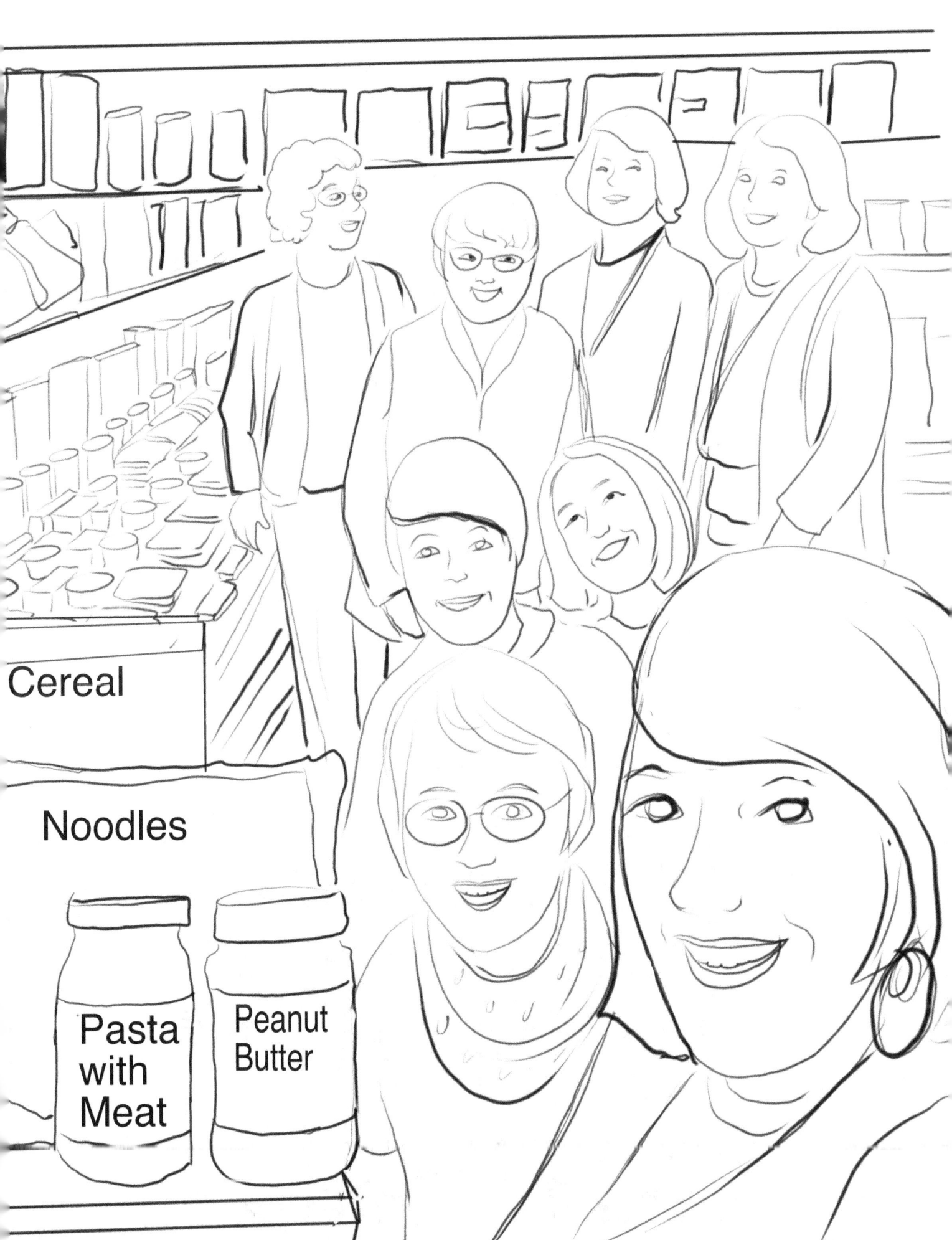

Cereal

Noodles

Pasta with Meat

Peanut Butter

Many homes have room for a horse or even two.

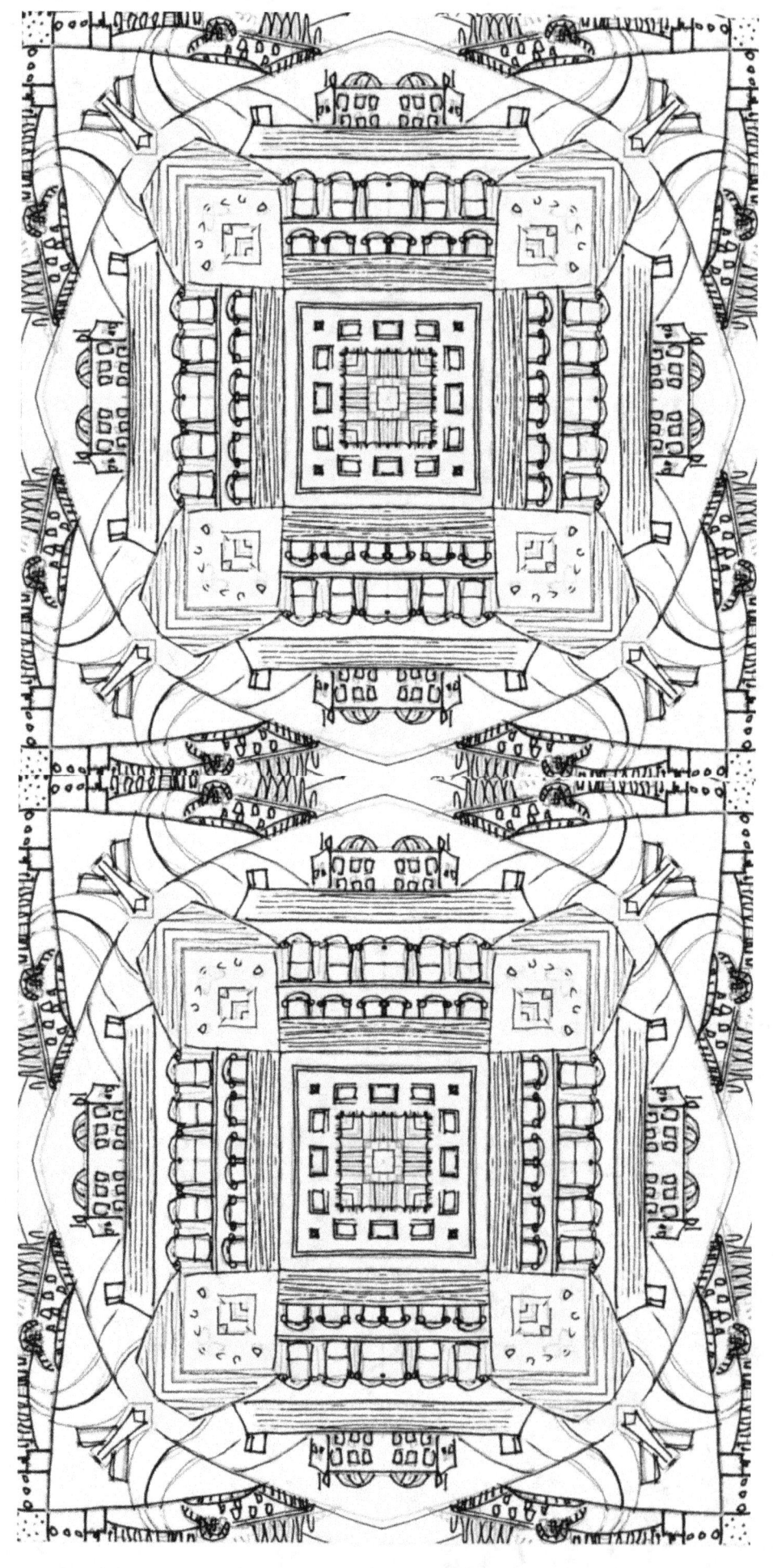

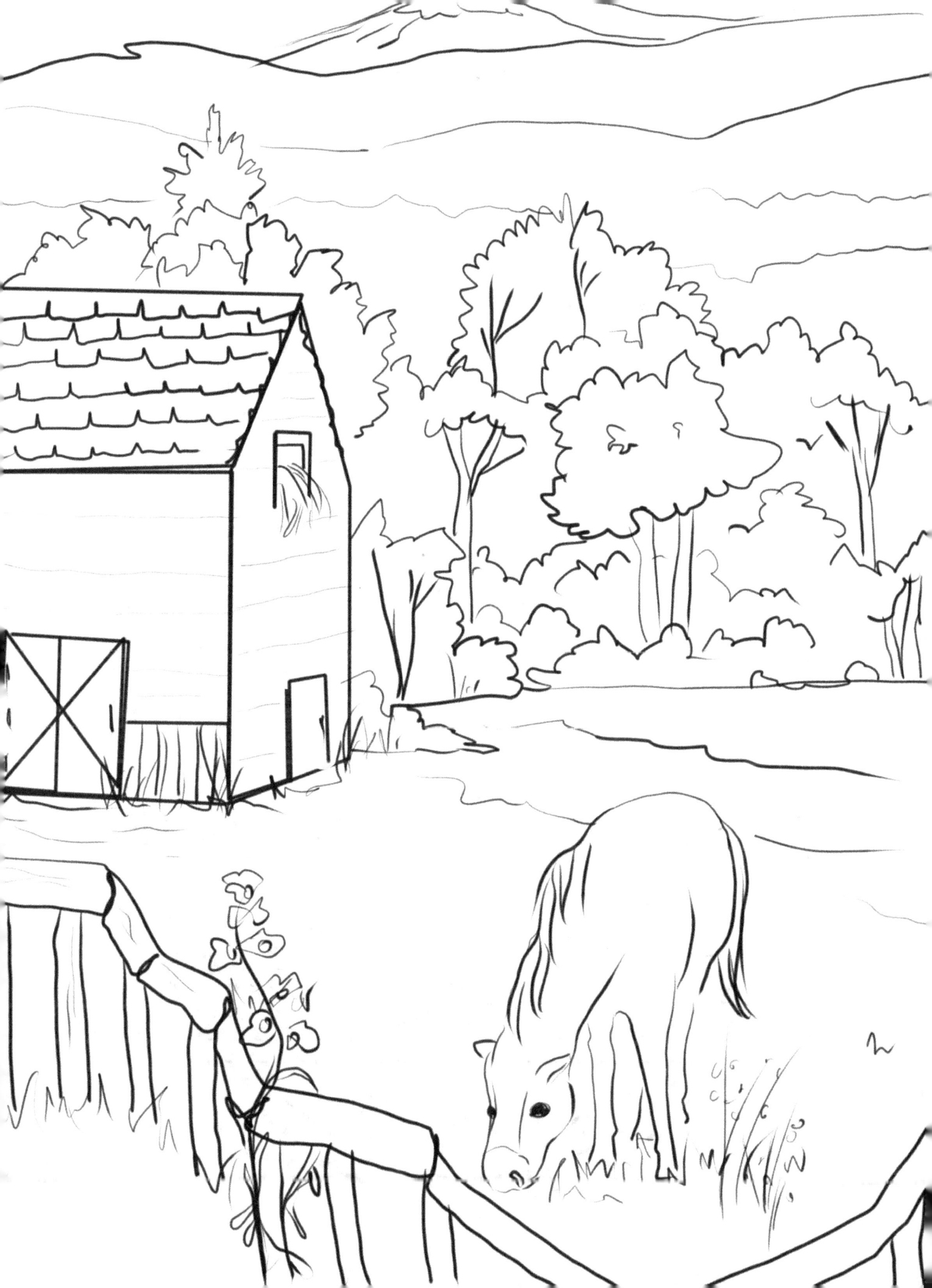

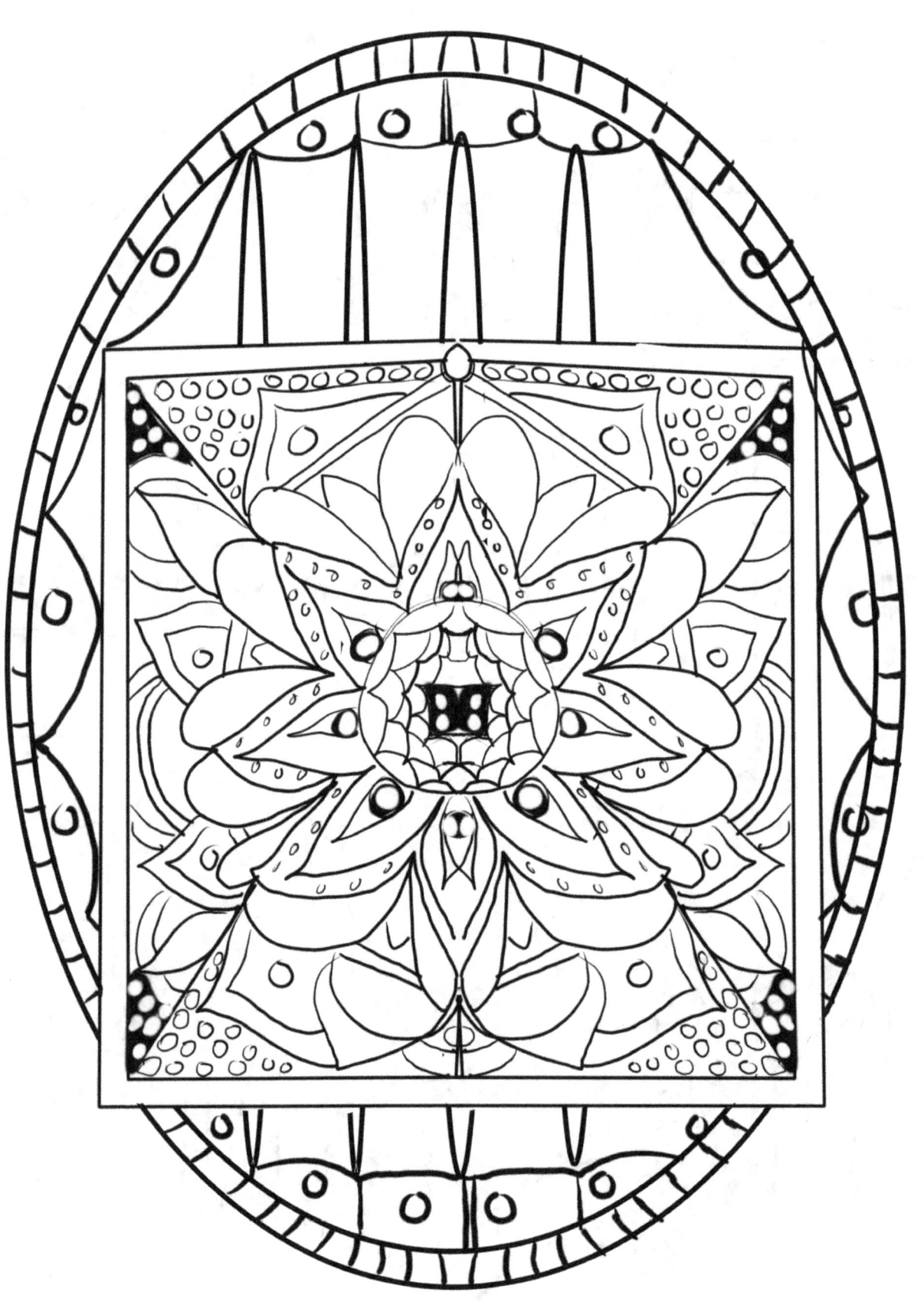

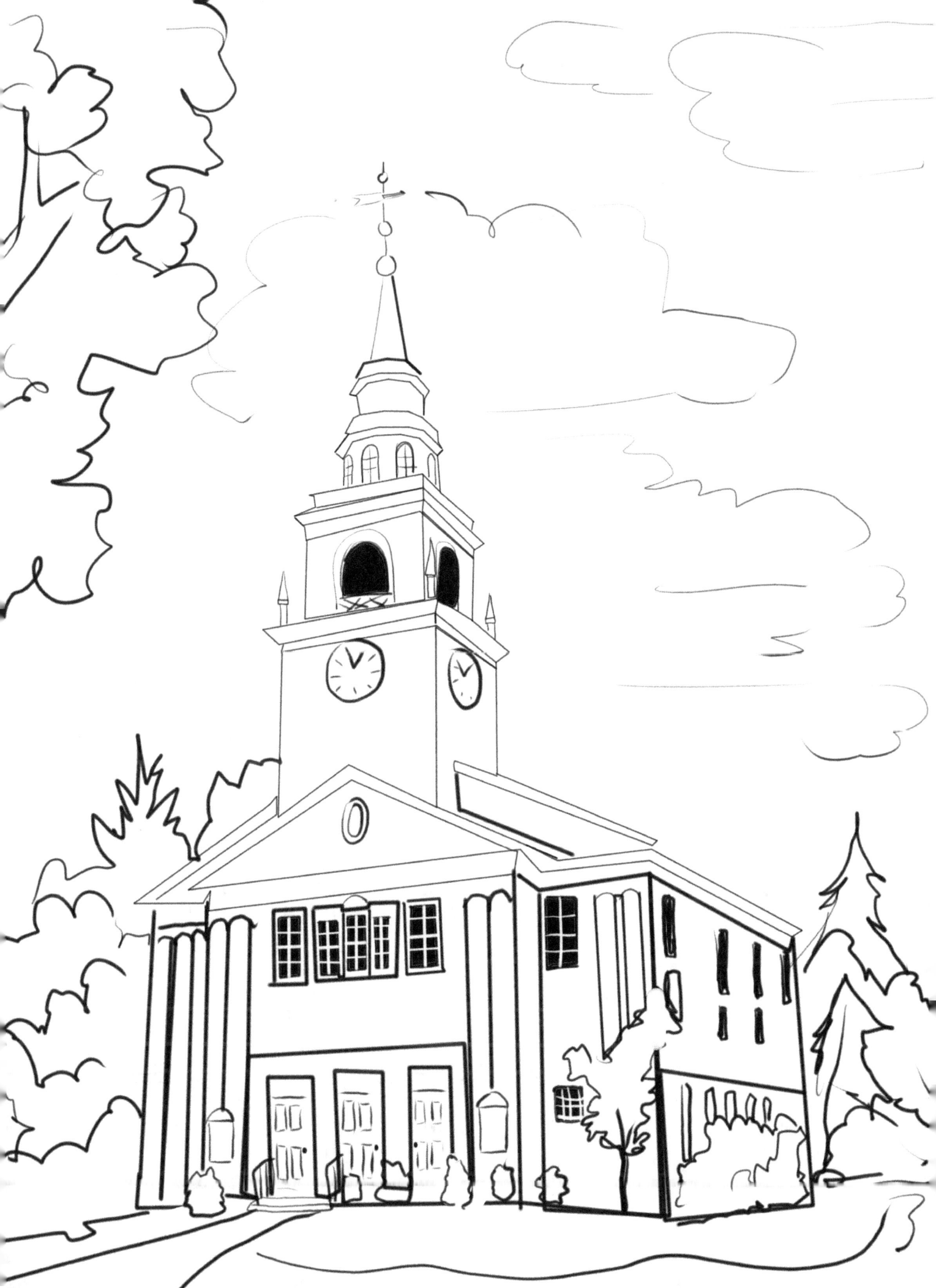

The Bennington, NH Library

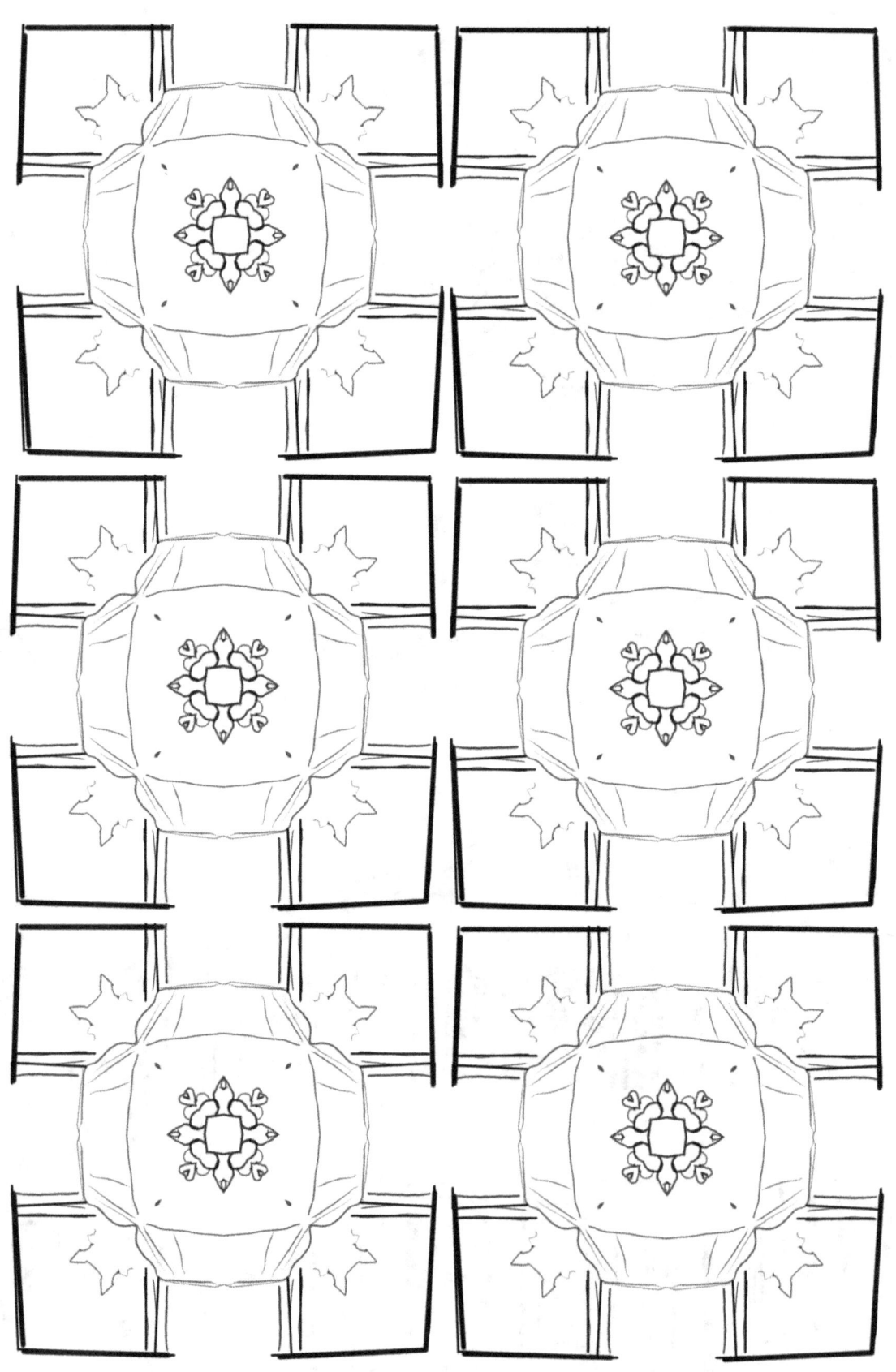

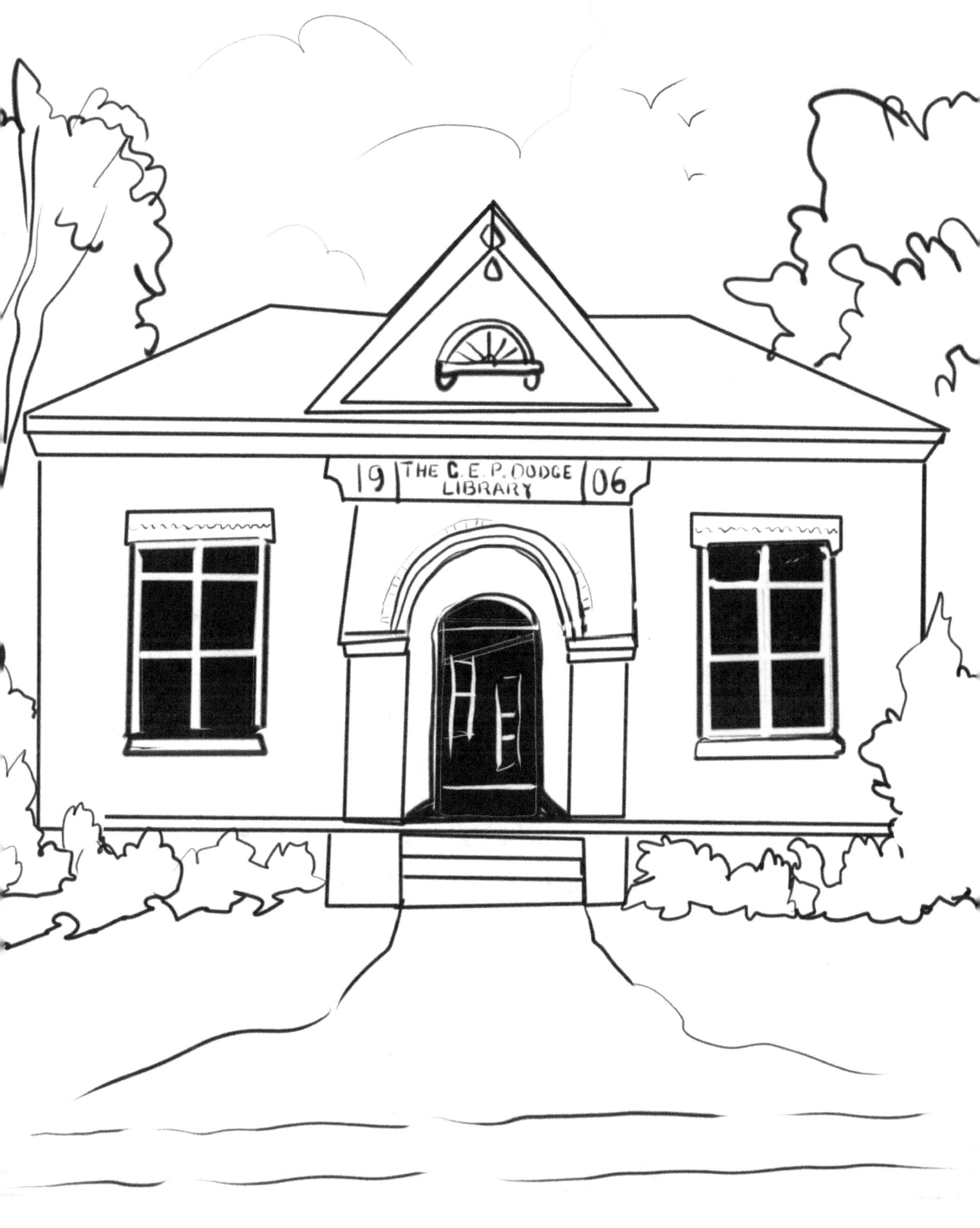

There is fun for everyone at the Peterborough Children and the Arts Day each May.

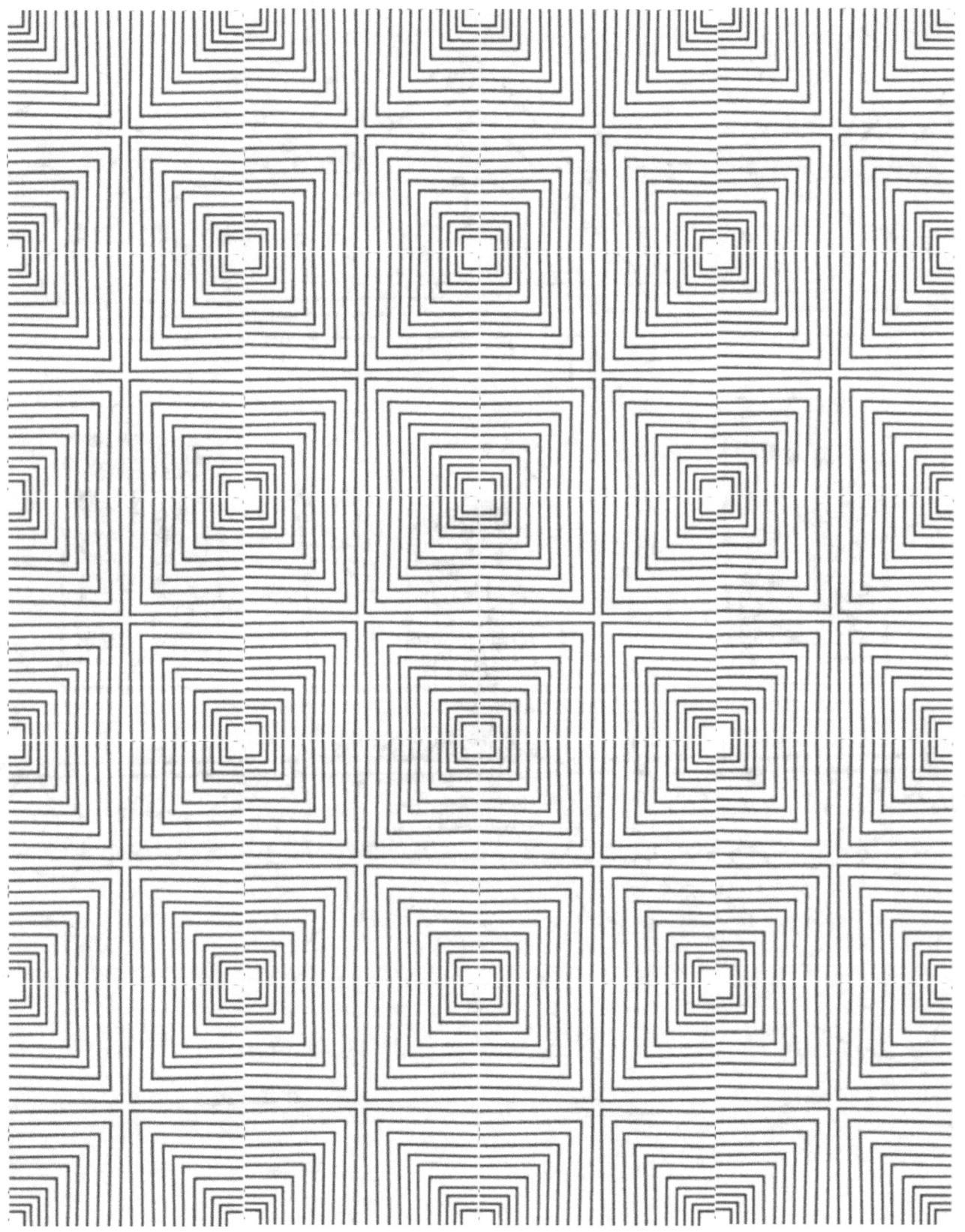

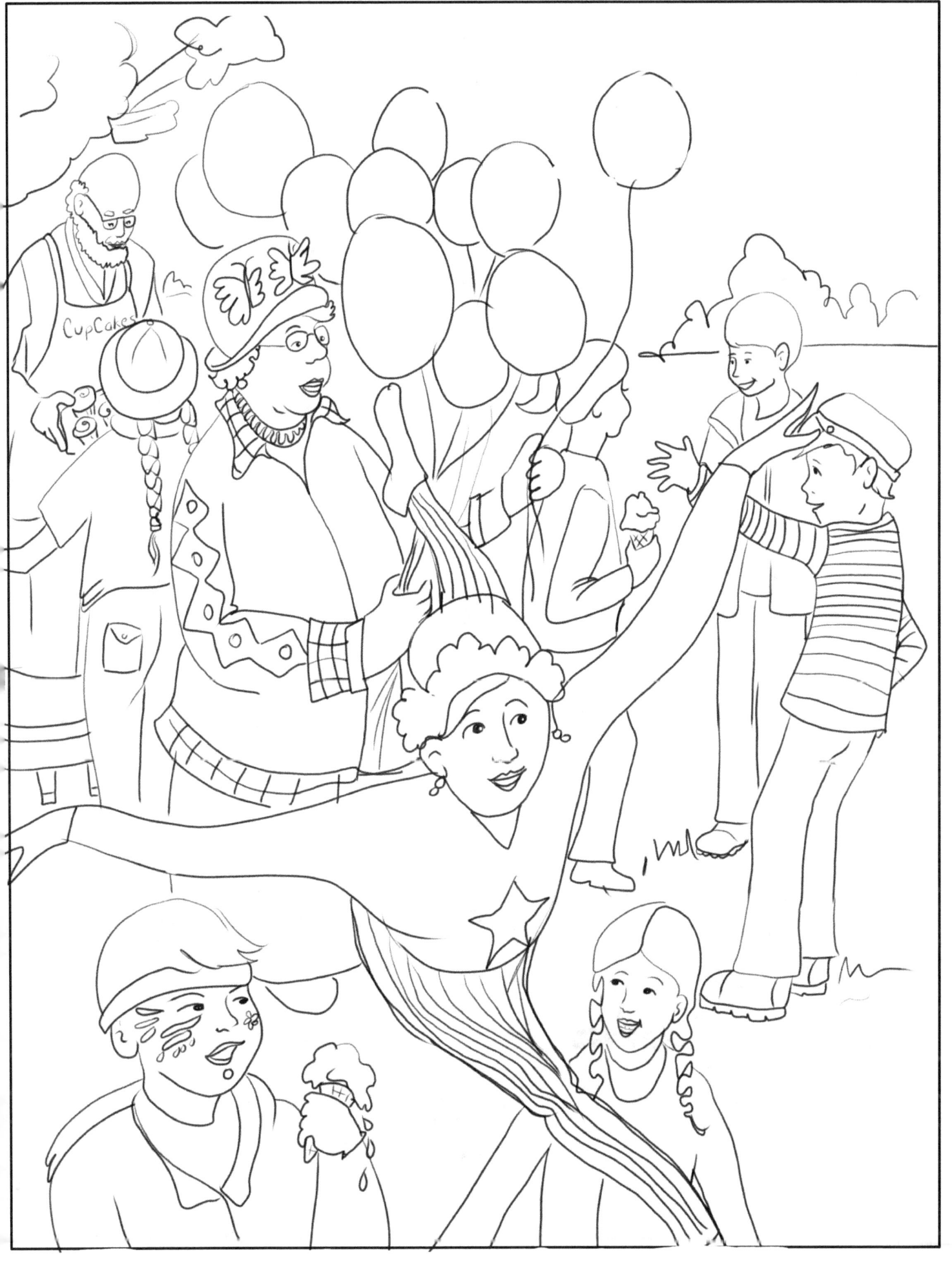

The Yankee Siege Castle in Greenfield is the site of the annual Punkin Chunkin festival.

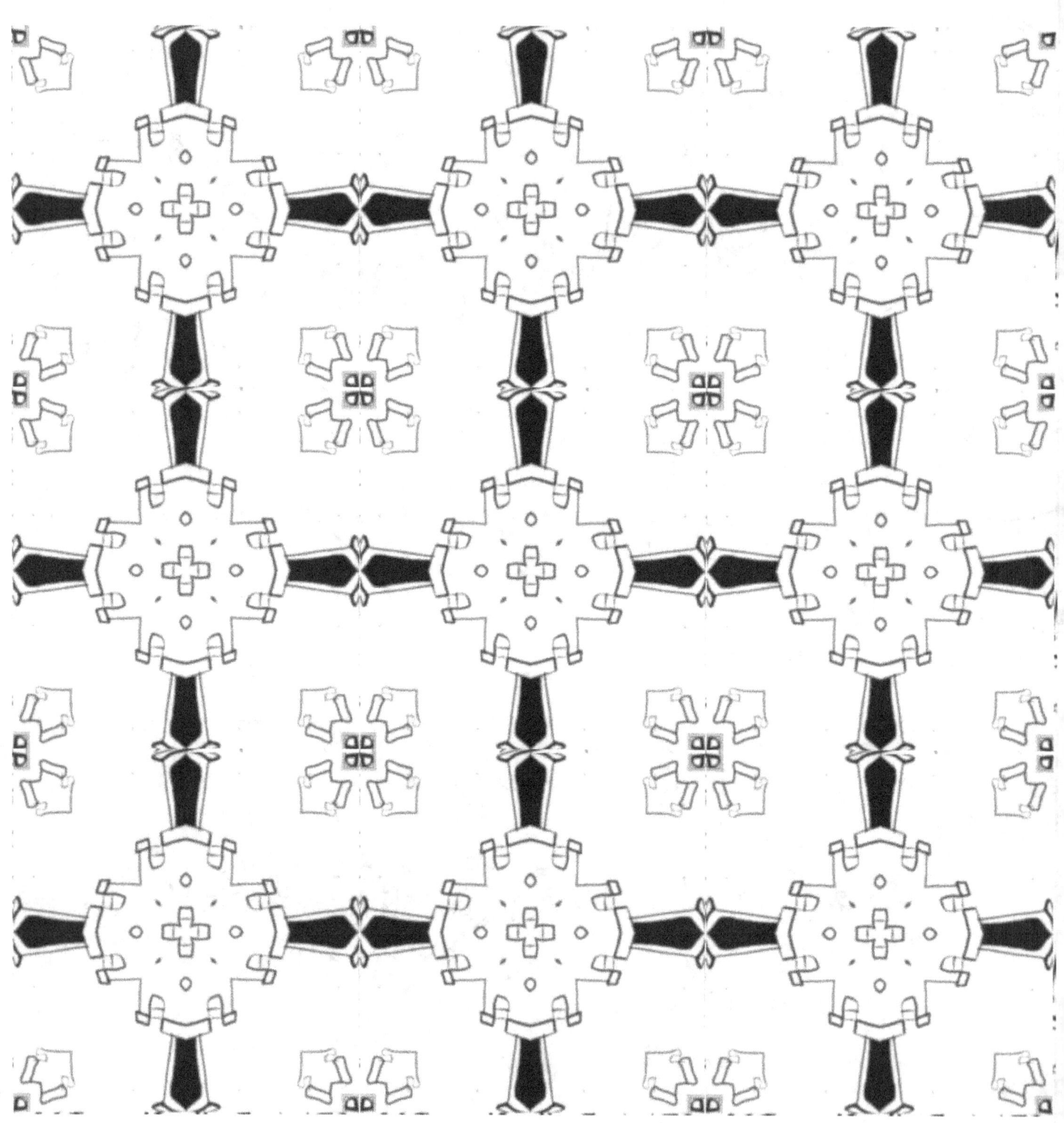

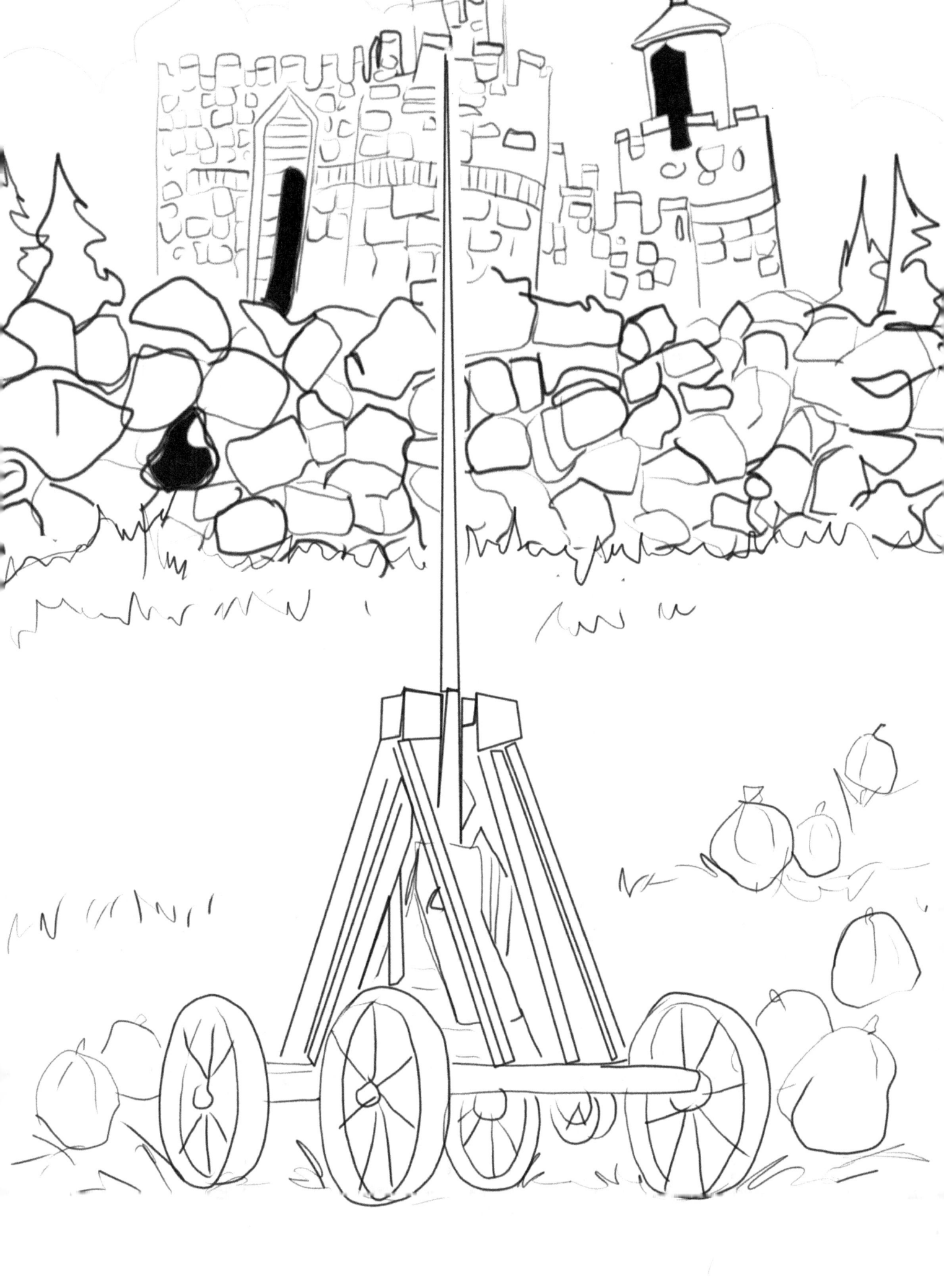

The Harris Center in Hancock, NH helps to create awareness of conservation.

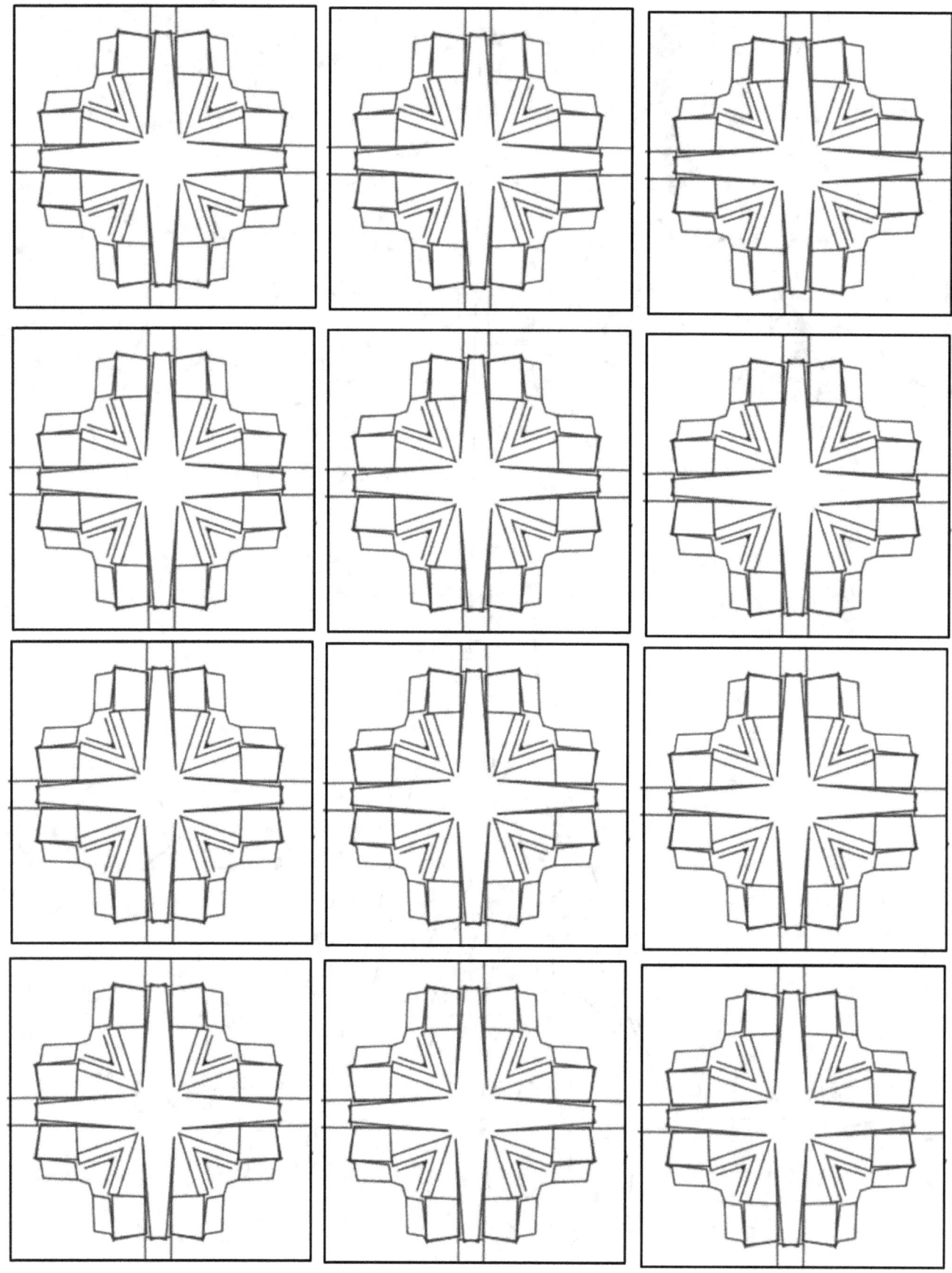

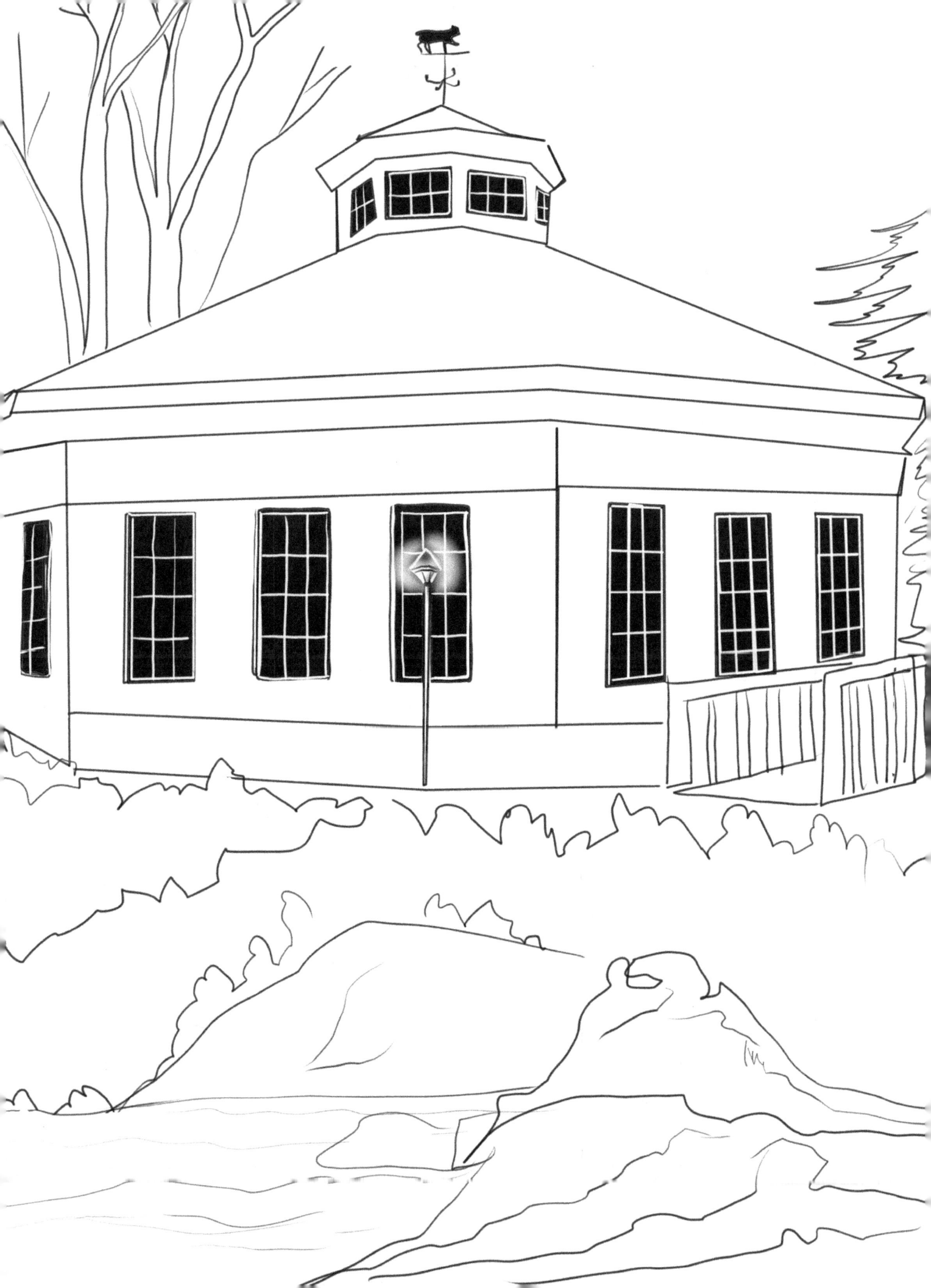

Families can enjoy the activities at Gregg Lake
in Antrim, NH. There are at least 959 lakes in NH.

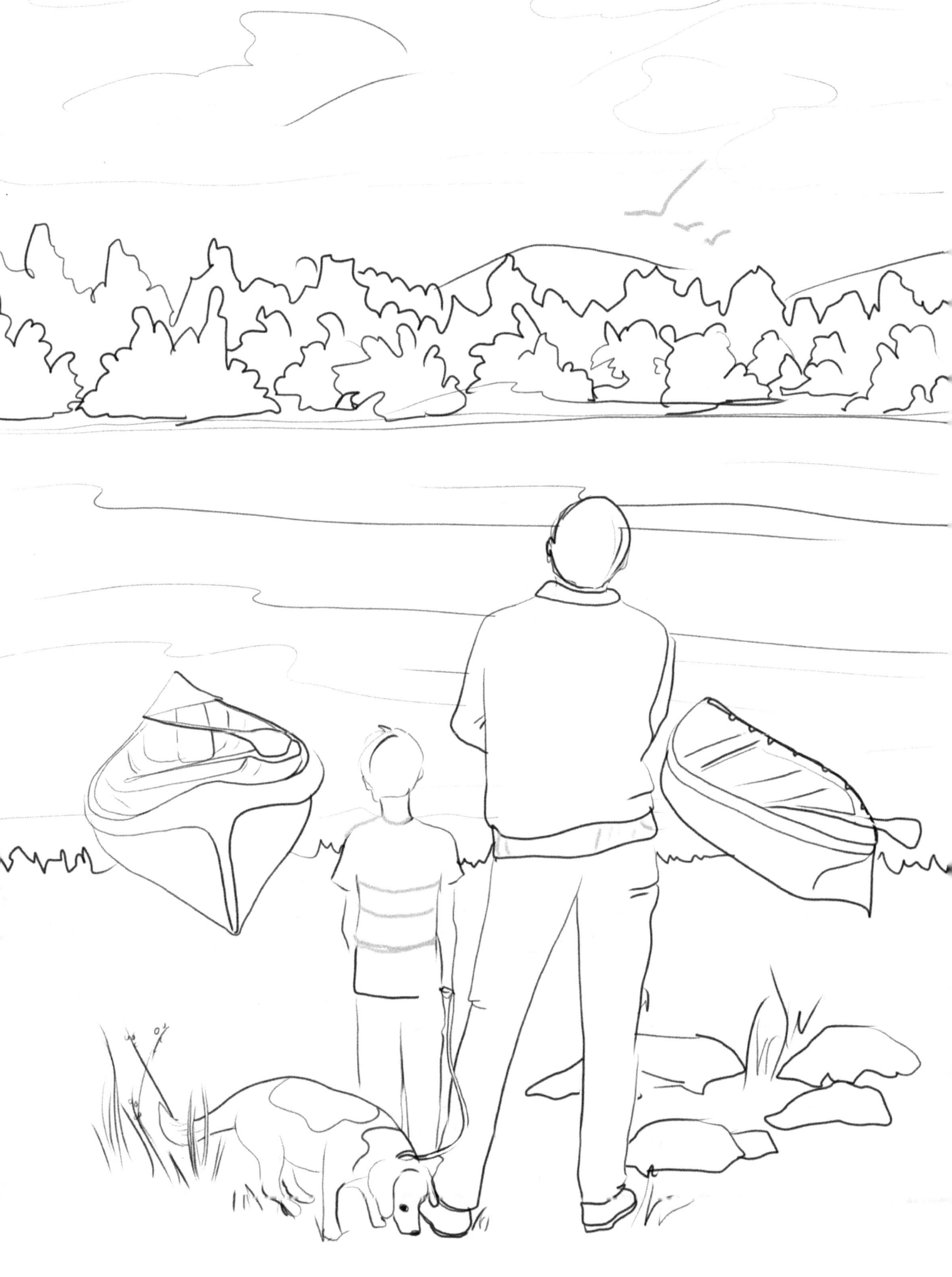

The Milford - Bennington Railroad

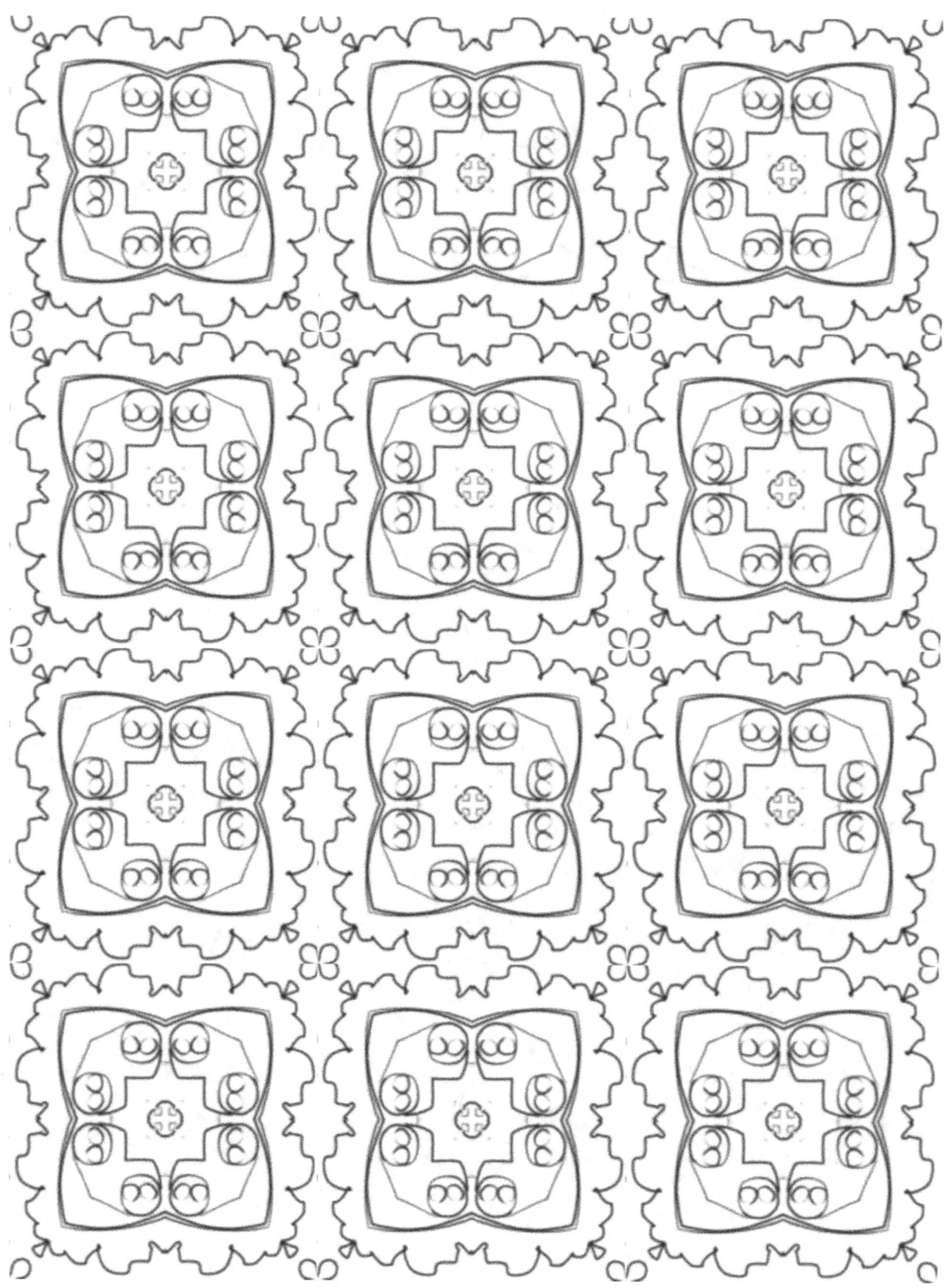

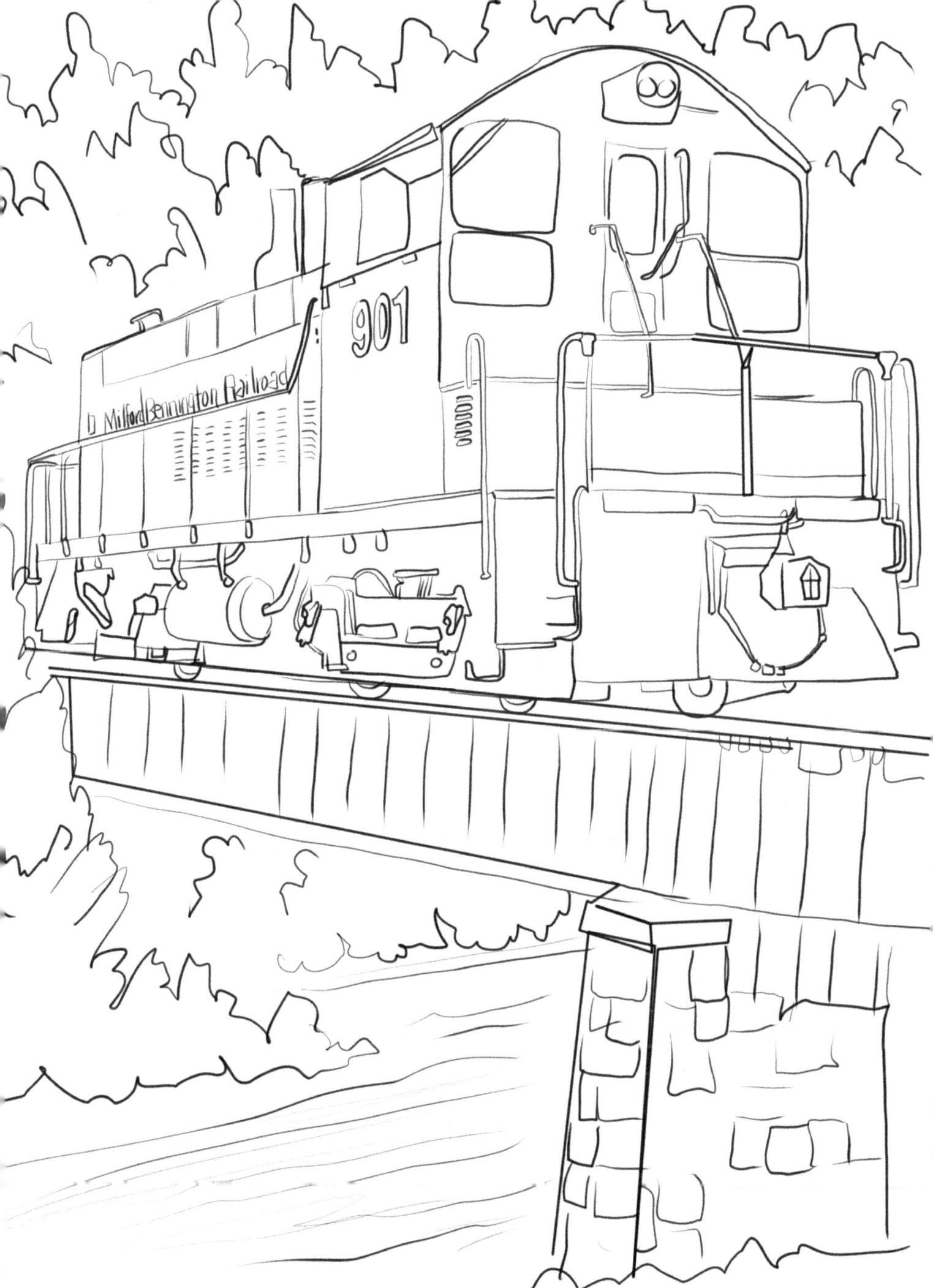

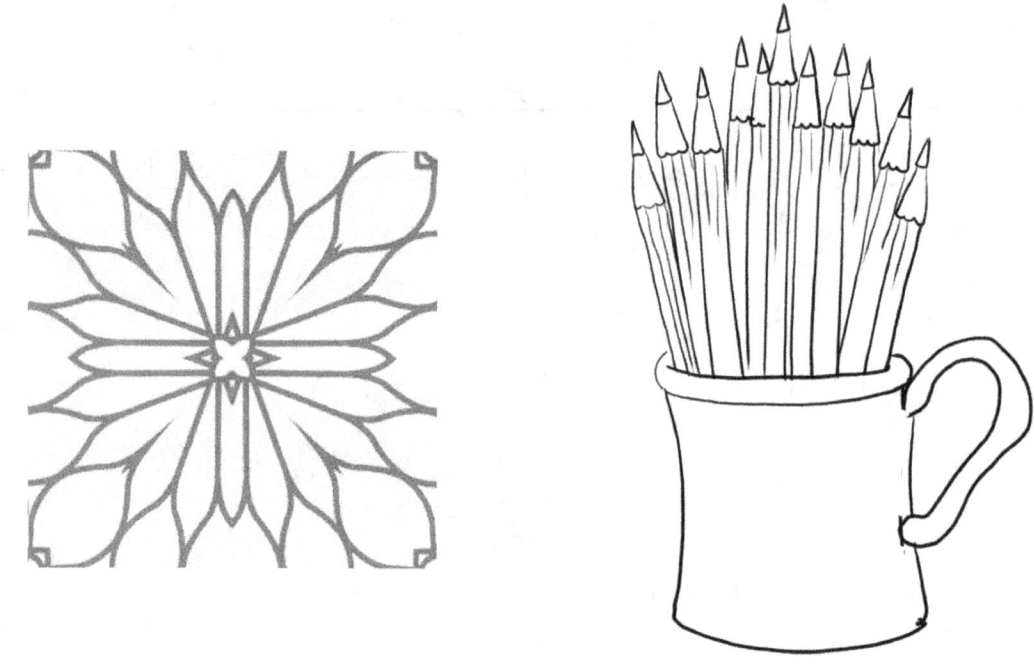

Suggestions for Coloring in this Book

It is a good idea to color with colored pencils only. That way none of the colors will bleed through to the back side of each page.

Since the line drawings allow for a full page of art the descriptions for the scenes are on the opposite design page.

You can use several colors with light pressure to create another color or enhance the shade of the piece you are coloring.